LEATHERHEADS
of the North

The True Story of Ernie Nevers & the Duluth Eskimos

CHUCK FREDERICK

X-comm

DULUTH, MINNESOTA

X-communication
The Carnegie Library
101 West Second Street, Suite 204
Duluth, Minnesota 55802
218-310-6541 • www.x-communication.org

Leatherheads of the north: the true story of Ernie Nevers and the Duluth Eskimos

Research assistance by Maryanne Norton, Carly Moritz, and Eric Faust.
Copy editing and additional research by Scott Pearson.
Cover and interior design and layout by Tony Dierckins.
Proof reading by Suzanne Rauvola and Julie Frederick.

Cover art by Tony Dierckins.
(Collage of historic, public domain images includes a detail
of a painting by Gary Thomas, used with permission.)

Eskimo "Igloo" logo © 2007 by X-Communication.
(Design based on a hand-drawn logo used by the 1926 Duluth Eskimos.)

Back cover image of Ernie Nevers from a 2003 United States Postal Service stamp.
Team photo from the Eskimos' 1926 training camp courtesy of the
Two Harbors Public Library and the Lake County Historical Society.

08 09 10 11 • 5 4 3 2

Library of Congress Control Number: 2007932040
ISBNs: 1-887317-32-5 & 978-1-887317-32-0

Printed in Brainerd, Minnesota, U.S.A., by Bang Printing.

For my arms-in-the-air, "TOUCHDOWN!"-shouting, green-and-gold-wearing Gal Pals: Claire, Charleigh, and Regine. All my love!

— C.F.

~

The publisher would like to thank:

Kris Aho and the crack reference staff of the Duluth Public Library,
Bob Carroll and the Professional Football Researchers Association,
the College Football Hall of Fame, Eric Faust, Julie Frederick,
Harry "Bud" Grant, the Green Bay Packers Hall of Fame Inc.,
Denis Gullickson, Tom Kasper, Bob King and the *Duluth News Tribune*,
the Lake County Historical Society, *Lake Superior Magazine*,
Rory Litwin and the University of Minnesota Duluth Library,
Pat Maus and the Northeast Minnesota Historical Center, Carly Moritz,
Bob Murphy, Maryanne Norton, Dick Palmer and the *Duluth Budgeteer*,
Scott Pearson, Michael Fabus and the Pittsburgh Steelers, Suzanne Rauvola,
Barry Singer, Marty Sozansky and the UMD Department of Composition,
Gary Thomas, the United States Postal Service,
and the Two Harbors Public Library.

The author's acknowledgments can be found on page 162.

Contents

A Place in History

Late in a game against the Green Bay Packers, the home team from Duluth, Minnesota—named for the hardware store that provided their red-and-white uniforms—trailed 0-6.

Time for a bit of trickery, the Kelley-Duluth team decided, even though anything other than a straight-ahead running play was considered reckless and unheard-of during the smash-mouth early days of the National Football League.

Quarterback Doc Kelly pulled aside one of his linemen, Howard Kiley, a native of Michigan. At 200 pounds, Kiley was considered a large man by early 1920s NFL standards. All day, he had been doing battle in the trenches against an even larger man, Green Bay's Cub Buck, who weighed 259 pounds. Kiley had to have been at least a little puzzled by Kelly's instructions.

"Line up eligible" to receive the ball, the quarterback said. "Cut in behind Buck [after he rushes in], and I'll lob you a pass." Kiley did as he was told, and the ball floated from the backfield and over the top of the charging Packers' tackle just as Kelly promised.

Kiley "caught the ball and took off down the sidelines," Duluth's legendary team owner Ole Haugsrud said, telling the story nearly thirty years later to *Duluth News Tribune* sportswriter Bruce Bennett. If Kiley scored, the team could take the game.

"But that wasn't enough for this big, good-natured guy," Haugsrud continued. "In those days, fans used to line up right along the sidelines to watch the game. Space in the grandstands was limited. As Kiley ran, he spotted, among the sideline spectators, Scotty Macaulay, for whom he did some boxing and wrestling around Duluth in the off-season.

"Kiley was quite a character. The fact that it was a close game and he was bound with the winning touchdown was no matter," Haugsrud said. "He paused momentarily, long enough to thumb his nose at Macaulay, before continuing on to score." The Kelleys won 7-6.

~

A great story. The early days of professional football are filled with such tales. However, as occasionally happens, the story doesn't completely jibe with official records. In the five years Duluth was a member of the NFL, from 1923 to 1927, its teams—Kelley-Duluth and later Ernie Nevers' Eskimos—played the Packers at home only one time, on September 28, 1924. Late in that game, Kelley-Duluth trailed 0-3, not 0-6, as Haugsrud recalled. Perhaps he was remembering some other exhibition or off-the-books non-league game between Green Bay and Duluth. Unofficial match-ups were common in those dizzying days of disorganization.

In the game of record, Kiley did not catch a long pass from Kelly. Rather, Jack Underwood, a hometown hero from Duluth Central High School, took a short pass near the sidelines from Cobb Rooney, another athlete bred in the forests and ore mines of the northern half of the Gopher State. According to the coverage of the game in the following morning's *News Tribune*, it was Underwood who raced along the sideline, slipping past a tackler and shaking off the Packers' famous Curly Lambeau before struggling over the goal line. He gave his Duluth "eleven" a 6-3 victory.

The paper didn't mention anything about Underwood or anyone else pausing to thumb a nose at a spectator.

And therein was one of the chief challenges in creating this book: separating romance from records and distinguishing folklore from fact in retelling stories born during sports' "golden age." Every anecdote was checked out before being included. The spelling of every name was double-checked and sometimes triple-checked. And the accuracy of every rushing record and other statistic was verified.

Fortunately, first-hand accounts of games and other information were still available on the microfilmed but long-forgotten pages of numerous newspapers. Accurate records and other facts were made abundantly available by the

National Football League, the Pro Football Hall of Fame, the College Football Hall of Fame, and other reliable sources.

Did a tall tale slip by? An embellishment? I wouldn't be surprised. But, for the most part, the accomplishments and accounts of football's pioneering days and of the game's pioneering characters checked out and were as true as a Brett Favre spiral, as accurate as a first-down chain gang, and as dependable as a marching band at halftime. The stories that didn't stand up to such scrutiny were left out.

∼

The overall story of the Duluth Eskimos is the story of the NFL's birth.

It's a story the league considered important enough that in 1963 Dick McCann, director of the about-to-open Pro Football Hall of Fame in Canton, Ohio, asked Haugsrud to fill a trunk of Eskimos mementos. Scouring his attic and the collections of fans and former players, Haugsrud gathered and donated pictures; papers; a replica No. 11 Ernie Nevers' Eskimos jersey; one of the extra-long mackinaw coats the Eskimos wore on the sidelines and while traveling; a pair of mud-splattered football pants worn by hall-of-fame halfback Johnny "Blood" McNally; a pair of football shoes used in games by Eskimos' center Bill Stein of Two Harbors, Minnesota; an old leather helmet; and other items.

"There's a story in every piece," Haugsrud said. He wrote that Stein "greased his elbows before every game so that opposing linemen would slide off without leaving a scratch."

The pieces—the "most fantastic collection of memorabilia in sports history," as McCann wrote shortly after the hall of fame's opening—helped to recreate a locker room scene at the hall of fame. The trunk is open. Football gear is spilling out. An exhausted player sits, hunched over on a bench.

"The result is one of the most dramatic displays in all museum history," McCann wrote. It "portrays the role that Minnesota and its mighty men played in the long-ago struggle to bring the game to its present great stature.

"The Duluth story captures the appreciation of every one of the thousands of visitors to this exciting new building," he continued. The Eskimos, he said, were "the National Football League's greatest road team…Ernie Nevers' team—and Johnny "Blood" McNally's first team—and Ole Haugsrud's team.

"Pro football's hall of fame has many interesting things to see," he wrote. "But none better than the Duluth story."

~

In the early 1990s, the "Duluth story" so enthralled *Sports Illustrated* writer Rick Reilly—a ten-time National Sportswriter of the Year—that he and Duncan Brantley, one of the magazine's fact-checkers, penned a screenplay based on the team. They called their romantic comedy *Leatherheads* for the helmets the players wore in the 1920s. They sold the movie-to-be to Universal Studios. And then they waited for it to hit the silver screen.

"There were all kinds of false starts," Reilly told me in a November 2006 interview for the *Duluth News Tribune*. Megastar actors like Michael Keaton, Mel Gibson, and Ray Liotta all picked up and ran with the script at different times, but always to no avail.

"None of it happened. It just sat. It's come very close," said Reilly. "It's such a fun story. [Our original screenplay] is set in Duluth and some in Chicago. Duluth played a big part in how the NFL took hold."

The movie finally did happen with Oscar-winner George Clooney tweaking the script and casting himself with Renee Zellweger in a "quick-witted romantic comedy set against the backdrop of America's nascent pro-football league in 1925," as Universal Pictures touted the film in the summer of 2007. "Clooney plays Dodge Connolly, a charming, brash football hero who is determined to guide his team from bar brawls to packed stadiums. But after the players lose their sponsor and the entire league faces certain collapse, Dodge convinces a college football star to join his ragtag ranks."

The story line mirrors reality; the NFL was facing the possibility of collapse when Haugsrud wooed college All-American Ernie Nevers to Duluth and to the NFL. And like Nevers, the movie's "favorite son"—Carter Rutherford, played by John Krasinski of TV's *The Office*—is golden-haired and with "dashing good looks and unparalleled speed on the field."

Zellweger, an Oscar winner herself, plays Lexie Littleton, "a cub journalist" and "spitfire newswoman." Clooney's and Krasinski's characters soon "become serious off-field rivals for her fickle affections." Hard to believe the dirt-and-blood story of the Duluth Eskimos and the untamed and unscrupulous early days of professional football included a love triangle. But that's Hollywood.

~

In 1963, around the same time a new football season was starting, the St. Louis County Historical Society, based in Duluth, decided to organize and host a ritzy reunion dinner for members of the old Eskimos teams. Haugsrud, former players, and others were invited to share their stories and their memories. The legacy of Duluth's NFL teams, for the first time, was celebrated in one place and at one moment.

Inside a packed Hotel Duluth ballroom, they reminisced about how the bigger-than-life Eskimos were treated like rock stars during their legendary barnstorming tour of 1926, how the crowds at the train stations were sometimes so large the team could hardly move, how their ranks included three future Pro Football Hall of Fame members, and how the team's owner was once credited for saving the National Football League. Nowadays it seems more than just a sports organization—the NFL is a way of life in America.

"The Eskimos are an important part of Duluth's sports history and were among the [pioneers] of the National Football League," Historical Society Director J. F. Robinson stated simply. "We feel that a preserved record of their days here is a must."

More than four decades later, I couldn't help but feel the same way.

— Chuck Frederick, July 23, 2007

THE BIRTH OF FOOTBALL
AND THE NFL

Football was an American invention. "The game, like the country in which it was created, was a rough, bastardized thing that jumped up out of the mud," Sally Jenkins wrote in *The Real All Americans*. "What was football but barely legalized fighting?" It evolved from rugby on East Coast college campuses in the 1880s, primarily through changes to the rules instituted by Walter Camp, the "Father of American Football." He played football at Yale from 1876 to 1881 and served on the rules committee for almost thirty years beginning in 1878. By 1883, American football was well on its way to being the game we recognize today.

The first documented football game in Duluth may have been on the Fourth of July in 1886; it could just as easily have been a soccer match. A newspaper account of that contest—between the Union Jacks and an unidentified "eleven" on an athletic field near where Chester Creek splashes into Lake Superior—wasn't real specific. But let's assume that with that nineteenth-century game, which ended in a scoreless draw, football had arrived in the bustling Great Lakes port at the western tip of Lake Superior.

Far from the high-flying, multimillion-dollar industry it is today, football in its infancy was a rough, crude, and slow-moving affair filled with drop kicks, bone-crunching line play, and wedges of grunting, muscular men pushing against each other to move a watermelon-sized oval toward a goal. Because the fatter ball was difficult to pass and could bounce and roll seemingly forever, punting was king and passing was odd. Punting was an offensive weapon, not a last resort for offensive failure. Teams routinely booted on third down to pin back their opponents. When teams did pass, the rules required them to heave the oval from at least five yards behind their line of scrimmage. Incomplete passes in the end zone resulted in turnovers.

When ball carriers were tackled out of bounds or near the sidelines, the ball wasn't brought back to the middle of the field or to the nearest hash mark for the next play. It was placed right there at the sidelines. Fields didn't have hash marks then. "The same man played offense and defense and there were few specialists," Erneste Cuneo, an All-American for Columbia University and a lineman for the 1929 Orange Tornadoes and 1930 Brooklyn Dodgers, once said. "In those days, the eleven played sixty minutes of football or until unconscious." That last part wasn't much of a joke. Football was bone-crushing dangerous in those early days, and annual death tolls were published and publicized. Between 1901 and 1907, 101 football deaths were tallied. That's about one death every three weeks.

~

Duluth's first high school contest likely took place on November 4, 1893, when the Duluth Central team squared off against a team from Minneapolis. The "inexperienced" Duluth team, as it was described in a news report, fell 26-8. After the game, Central's players and fans showed true class, though, demonstrating that football even in its infancy meant more than mud and sweat and could become part of a societal fabric. They hosted a reception and dance for the visiting team and its supporters, many of whom had piled into a northbound train to attend the game.

Central's heated rivals would come to include the Blaine and Nelson-Dewey high schools in neighboring Superior, Wisconsin. The gear was a far cry from today's space-age helmets and high-tech shoulder pads, rib protectors, and other protective wear. The players' "equipment would consist of little more than nose guards [and] shin guards…. Some wore tassel caps for headgear," the owner of Duluth's NFL team, the Duluth Eskimos, would write in 1963. "Some of the boys wore suits that looked as though they had been poured into them."

"Young fellows let their hair grow thick in the autumn to provide protection," the *Duluth News Tribune* claimed in 1956. "Rubber nose guards hung from a strap around the head and were clamped in the teeth to keep the nose from being broken. Slatted protectors were strapped on shins. Football pants were quilted."

Some players stuffed their heads into Zuppke helmets, which were little more than leather shells lined with slim pieces of padding. Far from insulting, calling them leatherheads seemed perfectly natural. They weren't playing soccer, after all.

~

The earliest known professional football—professional because a player was given money to play—occurred on November 12, 1892, in Pittsburgh, Pennsylvania. William "Pudge" Heffelfinger, a one-time standout at Yale, was paid $500 to play a single game for the Allegheny Athletic Association. In today's dollars, his payday was an amazing $10,820.

The first game in which all the players received payment was in 1895 in Latrobe, Pennsylvania. After that, "teams started organizing fast in western Pennsylvania and eastern Ohio. [The] Canton Bulldogs was one of the first teams in Ohio," according to legendary Eskimos owner and manager Ole Haugsrud.

The Duluth-Superior area's first semi-pro teams started around 1910 with balls and protective gear borrowed from high schools and neighborhood teams. Battles between the Superior Badgers and Big Duluth were reunions of sorts, as many players were former standouts from Central, Blaine, and Nelson-Dewey.

"I was just a little kid at the time and more concerned about carrying Dave Bancroft's bat into Hislop Park [in Superior] than seeing football games," Haugsrud wrote, explaining that baseball was far and away the sport of choice back then; Bancroft was a local hero who became a Major League Hall of Famer.

In 1915 a semi-pro football team organized in Duluth's West End called the Adams Athletic Club (the club also promoted baseball and hockey). The Adams played teams from Superior and from Northeastern Minnesota's Mesabi Iron Range.

Frank "Cub" La Joy led a Duluth City Team. All the players were local, but the Duluth team had a ringer: University of Minnesota fullback Lorin Solon. Across the Duluth-Superior Harbor, the Superior YMCA sponsored a team in Billings Park, and a Superior City Team formed in 1916. In addition to the two city teams playing each other—with trainloads of enthusiastic fans zipping between Duluth and Superior to attend each contest—they also did battle with the St. Paul Banholzers, the Minneapolis Marines, and other elevens from the Twin Cities and its suburbs.

The makeshift semi-pro clubs broke up as the nation entered World War I, but the war didn't stop football in Duluth. In shipyards that employed thousands and would produce 103 vessels for the war effort, a semi-pro league formed. Some of its players would eventually become the nucleus of Duluth's NFL teams. They included Dewey Scanlon, who played quarterback for Valparaiso University in Indiana; Wally Gilbert, a Duluth Denfeld High School graduate and fullback and halfback for Valparaiso; Alfred Clarke, a halfback, quarterback, and tackle for Nevada-Reno; and Dick O'Donnell, a standout halfback for Duluth Denfeld High School. Another shipyard league player was Harry Grant, the father of legendary Minnesota Vikings coach Bud Grant.

~

Pro football not only was rough, dirty, and unrespected, it also was, in its earliest days, horribly disorganized. College athletes used pseudonyms in order to illegally take pay to play, players jumped from team to team, chasing the highest offers. The rules of individual pro games changed from field to field. Officials favored the home teams that were paying their salaries. And every team was responsible for scheduling its own games.

Hoping to give order to the chaos, on the sweaty evening of September 17, 1920, the leaders of eleven pro teams—including George "Papa Bear" Halas of the Decatur Staleys, and representatives of the Canton Bulldogs, Racine Cardinals, Akron Pros, Cleveland Indians, Dayton Triangles, Massillon Tigers, Hammond Pros, Muncie Flyers, Rock Island Independents, and Rochester Jeffersons—piled into the Hupmobile car dealership in Canton, Ohio, owned by Ralph Hay, the Bulldogs' owner. Over beer and stories of gridiron greatness, they defined rules, traded ideas, elected a board, and created a professional league they called the American Professional Football Association. (Only two of the original franchises still exist today. The Decatur Staleys moved to Chicago in 1921, were renamed the Bears a year later, and are still a Chicago fixture. The Racine Cardinals, through a series of moves and name changes, became today's Arizona Cardinals. The Hupmobile auto showroom which gave birth to the league was located in a structure called the Odd Fellows Building which has since been razed. The spot is designated with an interpretive marker.)

Contrary to popular and oft-repeated claims, especially in Minnesota, neither Duluth nor Minneapolis were inaugural cities in the new league, and neither was Green Bay, Wisconsin, the home of the Packers. Before the new league officially began play, the Massillon, Ohio, Tigers decided against joining. Meanwhile, the Buffalo All-Americans, Chicago Tigers, Columbus Panhandles, and Detroit Heralds all wanted in and were welcomed. Every team in the new league was charged a $100 franchise fee, but the assessment mostly was to give the appearance of respectability. No team ever paid.

The first president of the American Professional Football Association was Jim Thorpe, the most famous athlete of the time, which gave the new league instant credibility. As a teenager at Carlisle Industrial Indian School in Pennsylvania—his mother was a descendant of Black Hawk, the last great chief of the Sauk and Fox, and a noted warrior and athlete—he begged iconic football legend Glenn "Pop" Warner for the opportunity to play varsity football. Warner resisted, telling Jim he was too small. Warner secretly didn't want to risk losing the school's best track prospect to a football injury. One day, Warner relented, however, and gave Thorpe the ball for an open-field drill. Thorpe outraced and outmaneuvered the varsity squad, Warner remembered, "like they were old maids." Warner would later look back and say it had been "an exhibition of athletic talent that I had never before witnessed, nor was I ever to again see anything similar."

Thorpe played his first college game on October 26, 1907, when his team's veteran halfback wrenched his knee and had to leave the game. The following two years he was selected as a third-team All-American in football. In 1910, he earned a spot on the first team. At the 1912 Olympics, he blew away the decathlon and pentathlon fields. Sweden's King Gustav V presented Thorpe with a gold medal, a wreath, and a jeweled gold-and-silver chalice shaped like a Viking ship, saying, "Sir, you are the greatest athlete in the world."

Thorpe's reply was as simple as his roots. "Thanks, King."

After the Olympics, however, he had his gold medals stripped from him after it was determined he had played semi-pro baseball for two seasons. (The medals would be returned posthumously in 1982.) Thorpe next played big-league baseball for the New York Giants and Boston Braves. He played professional football beginning in 1919 for the Canton Bulldogs. A year later he was president of the American Professional Football Association.

~

On September 26, 1920, the first game featuring a team from the new league was played at Douglas Park in Rock Island, Illinois. About eight hundred fans watched the Independents beat up on the St. Paul Ideals, 48-0.

A week later, league teams battled each other for the first time. The Dayton Triangles shut out the Columbus Panhandles, 14-0, in Triangle Park. Lou Partlow of Dayton scored the first touchdown in NFL history.

By December, most of the teams in the league had abandoned their quest for the season's championship. Some, including the Chicago Tigers and Detroit Heralds, had wrapped their seasons, ceased operations, and had their franchises canceled by the league.

Another team, Akron, sold tackle Bob Nash to Buffalo for $300 and five percent of the gate receipts: the league's first player deal.

No official standings were maintained that inaugural season, and teams played both league and non-league games. At a league meeting on April 30, 1921, the championship was awarded to the Akron Pros which reported winning eight games, losing none, and tying three times. The Decatur Staleys, at ten wins, one loss, and two ties, finished in second place. The Buffalo All-Americans, with nine wins, one loss, and one tie, were third. The Racine Cardinals and Rock Island Independents, both at six wins, two losses, and two ties, tied for fourth. The Dayton Triangles, with five wins, two losses, and two ties, were sixth. The Rochester (New York) Jeffersons, with six wins, three losses, and two ties, were seventh. The Canton Bulldogs, with seven wins, four losses, and two ties, were eighth. The Detroit Heralds, with two wins, three losses, and two ties, were ninth. The Cleveland Tigers, at two wins, four losses, and two ties, were tenth. The Chicago Tigers, two wins, five losses, and one tie, were eleventh. The Hammond Pros, two wins and five losses, were twelfth. The Columbus Panhandles, at two wins, six losses, and two ties, were thirteenth. And the Muncie Flyers, with one loss and only one game played, finished in last place.

Unofficially. Remember, the league didn't maintain standings.

~

Jim Thorpe was replaced as president of the American Professional Football Association after only one year. Joe Carr of the Columbus Panhandles was named to the position in 1921, with Carl Storck of Dayton chosen as secretary-treasurer. Carr moved the league's headquarters to Columbus, Ohio. He drafted a league constitution and by-laws, gave teams territorial rights, restricted player movements, developed membership criteria for franchises, and issued standings for the first time, so that the league would have a clear champion.

The league grew from fourteen teams to twenty-two in 1921. John Clair of the Acme Packing Company in Green Bay, Wisconsin, was awarded one of the new franchises. His team was named the Packers. Minnesota also became part of the league with the Minneapolis Marines. The other new teams included the Evansville Crimson Giants, the Washington Senators, Cincinnati Celts, Tonawanda Kardex, Louisville Brecks, and New York Giants. The Cleveland Tigers changed their name to the Cleveland Indians. Player-coach Frederick "Fritz" Pollard of the Akron Pros was the league's first African-American head coach. The Decatur Staleys were turned over by A. E. Staley to George Halas. Staley paid Halas $5,000 to keep the team name for one more season. Halas, with halfback Ed "Dutch" Sternaman as his partner, moved the team to Cubs Park in Chicago.

The Chicago Staleys and Buffalo All-Americans finished the season with identical records of nine wins and one loss. But because Buffalo tied twice and Chicago only once, the league championship was awarded by Carr to the Staleys, giving Halas his first league championship. The Packers finished seventh with three wins, two losses and one tie. The Minneapolis Marines were fifteenth with one win and three losses.

～

The American Professional Football Association changed its name to the National Football League, or NFL, on June 24, 1922. The comings and goings of franchises continued in the new year, the league dropping from twenty-two teams to eighteen.

New were the Toledo Maroons, who'd go on to have a good year in 1922, winning five times, losing twice and tying twice; the Racine Legion of Illinois, who'd also have a good season, winning six times, losing four games, and tying once; the Milwaukee Badgers, who'd win twice, lose four times, and tie three games; and the Oorang Indians, who'd finish the season with three wins and six losses.

There were also some new names for returning teams. Chicago Staleys owner George Halas switched to the Chicago Bears. With the entry of the Racine Legion, the Racine Cardinals decided to become the Chicago Cardinals.

Gone from the 1921 campaign were the Cleveland Indians, Detroit Heralds, Muncie Flyers, New York Giants, and three teams that played just one season: the Washington Senators, who won once against two losses in 1921; the Cincinnati Celts, who won once and lost three times; and the Tanawanda Kardex, who played only one game during its one season. The Kardex lost it.

Nearly gone in 1922 were the Green Bay Packers, who admitted to, and were reprimanded for, using college players. Crackdowns had been launched by the new league.

On January 28, John Clair of the Acme Packing Company withdrew from the league. Green Bay player and coach Curly Lambeau refused to let the team die, however. The legend-in-the-making promised to obey league rules, and he put up $50 of his own money to buy back the franchise.

That wasn't the end of tough times for the Packers in 1922. Bad weather and low attendance plagued the reorganized team, and Lambeau went broke. This time, local merchants came to the rescue, arranging a $2,500 loan and setting up a public nonprofit corporation to operate the team. The Packers today remain the NFL's only publicly owned franchise.

The Canton Bulldogs won the league championship in 1922, finishing undefeated with ten wins and two ties. They were led by player-coach Guy Chamberlin and tackles Link Lyman and Wilbur "Pete" Henry. The Pro Football Hall of Fame dubbed the 1922 Bulldogs "the league's first true powerhouse."

The Bears finished second with nine wins and three losses. The Packers were eighth with four wins, three losses, and three ties. Wisconsin's other team, the Milwaukee Badgers, were in eleventh place with two wins, four losses, and three ties. And Minnesota's team, the Minneapolis Marines, finished thirteenth with one win and three losses.

~

The big business of college football in the 1920s was dominated by Harvard, Princeton, Yale, and Columbia, the four schools that formed the Intercollegiate Football Association in 1876. "Back then college football was all the rage, and this new pro thing was just a fad in most people's eyes," according to Ross Bernstein, author of *Pigskin Pride*. "There was even an assumption and an unwritten rule then that if you played professionally, you could never get a college coaching job. Chicago University coach Amos [Alonzo] Stagg went a step further, declaring that if any of his boys went on to play professionally after graduation he would revoke their varsity letter."

On one occasion, Stagg and his team were travelling east by train to a game against Princeton. The Chicago Cardinals, on their way to play in New

York, were on the same train. "The Chicago University players were great admirers of the boys playing for a salary," Haugsrud recounted. "This irked Coach Alonzo Stagg to the point where he asked the train conductor to lock the doors between the coaches."

Understandably, college players eager for paychecks at the pro level played under assumed names. And pro owners, eager for the best talent the college ranks could offer, were more than happy to look the other way. "The college boys would play for their alma mater on Saturday and on Sunday they would play under an assumed name in some other city for a semi-pro football team," Haugsrud wrote. Bill Stein explained, "That was OK in those days. Everybody did it. Why, I remember some colleges used to pay the backs $100 for every touchdown."

Stein knew first hand. He had been drafted out of high school by a scout for Fordham University in New York. The scout, a native of Duluth's West End, had rounded up four Duluth-area athletes to play for Fordham. Three of them would return to help establish Duluth's NFL teams: Art "The Swede" Johnson, Bill Stein, and Lief Richard Strand. Before returning to Duluth, they'd play for Fordham on Saturdays, and on Sundays, their coach, the famous former drop kicker from Harvard, Charlie Brickley, would take them and the rest of his collegiate athletes to nearby Patterson, New Jersey, where they'd play professionally under assumed names.

Haugsrud recalled other instances of this practice, including one pro game in the coal regions of Illinois. Notre Dame's players, under the name of Carbondale, took on the entire Illinois team, which wore the jerseys of Coaldale. In Detroit another time, the University of Michigan team played under the name of the Detroit Heralds against the Ohio State team, which played under the name of the Toledo Mud Hens.

College football was big business, and the pros were emerging. But all of it was being marred by illegal practices and the way unsavory activities were so often excused with winks and turns of heads. The widespread deceit didn't last forever, of course, but long enough to become part of the lore of early football. The wrongdoings may be regarded with nostalgia now, but back then, eventually, there was a crackdown. "Many of the boys were reprimanded and were expelled from their various schools. Coaches were likewise given a lesson," Haugsrud wrote. "George Trafton, former Notre Dame center, was playing with the Chicago Bears and coaching the line at Northwestern, and he, along with many others who played professional ball on Sunday were [eventually] told to make their choice: either college or pro football."

~

Meanwhile, interest in football in the Twin Ports remained strong. In 1922, a team formed in Superior called the Christies. A Christies player named Ole Sorenson made his semi-pro football debut by accidentally scoring for the opposing team. The team had traveled to Superior from Ironwood, Michigan, for the game. And across the lake, a team from Duluth was taking shape as 1922 turned into 1923. The Marines wouldn't be Minnesota's lone NFL team for long.

ONE

THE KELLEYS
TAKE THE FIELD

Professional football in Duluth got its start in a Superior Street hardware store in 1923. Kelley Hardware had been incorporated by pioneering industrialists Michael Hugh Kelley of Duluth, John F. Killorin of Swan River, Minnesota, and George W. Welles of Duluth on July 2, 1896. Kelley Hardware became a regular sponsor of amateur and semi-pro teams in the Duluth area, and in 1923, the store struck a sponsorship deal that would seal its legacy.

The manager of Kelley Hardware's sporting goods department, Marshall C. Gebert, inked the deal in partnership with three up-and-coming football stars: Dan Williams, a center from St. Cloud, Minnesota; Dewey Scanlon of West Duluth, fresh off his quarterbacking days at Valparaiso University in Indiana; and Joey Sternaman, a star for the University of Illinois.

The four partners entered Duluth in the National Football League, putting up $250 each to cover the league's $1,000 admission fee. The Kelley-Duluth franchise became official on July 28, 1923. Kelley Hardware provided the red-and-white jerseys—and the team's name. Gebert served as coach.

"Duluth's entry into the whirl of pro football was made during one of the wildest periods in the nation's history," according to Haugsrud, who would take ownership of the team in 1926. "Money was liquid in Duluth in those days. Store buildings and office rooms were at a premium. All industries were going to capacity. It was a propitious time for venture into the unknown realms of a major athletic pastime."

The four partners weren't the only ones eager for such a venture. More than one hundred semi-pro football players and former prep stars from Northeastern Minnesota and Northwestern Wisconsin turned out for tryouts for the Kelley-Duluth team, each of them hoping to recapture glory days by landing one of sixteen available roster spots.

The lineup card would wind up being filled with local boys, with one exception: Sternaman. He had been "brought here to direct the Kelleys," Haugsrud wrote. He was a "grand little quarterback who had achieved an enviable reputation as a drop kicker and field general" at Illinois. Born February 1, 1900, in Springfield, Illinois, where he played his high school ball, Sternaman played sixteen games for the Chicago Bears in 1922 and 1923 prior to his arrival in Duluth. With Kelley-Duluth, he "proved a big drawing card, delighted the customers with his staccato signal calling and his educated toe in lifting the pigskin over the goal post bar for the needed points in close contests," Haugsrud wrote.

Fellow team founder Dan "Doc" Williams was "a giant center who knew all the answers in the pivot spot," according to Haugsrud. Standing six feet seven inches tall and weighing 216 pounds, Williams was one of the largest athletes ever to play professionally in Duluth. A product of Minnesota's St. Cloud State University, he suited up for six Kelley-Duluth games in 1923 at the age of twenty-four.

Dewey Scanlon would play halfback for the new Kelley-Duluth team and serve as team manager. A natural athlete of five feet nine inches and 192 pounds, he learned the game in the sandlots of West Duluth before honing his skills at Valparaiso. He was born in Duluth in 1899.

～

Duluth was one of three new NFL franchises in 1923. The Cleveland Indians and St. Louis All-Stars also joined, while the Evansville Crimson Giants ceased operations. The total number of teams increased from eighteen to twenty. Two teams changed names: Columbus from Panhandles to Tigers and Akron from Pros to Indians. For the first time, all the franchises considered members of the NFL would play league games. Since each team still set its own schedule, Canton, Milwaukee, and the two teams from Chicago, the Bears and Cardinals, would end up playing twelve league games while the Rochester Jeffersons would play only two.

Jim Thorpe remained the biggest star in the league, returning for his second and final season with the Oorang Indians. A single play typified the disappointing year he had. Trailing 26-0 to the Bears, Oorang was on the verge of a touchdown, a momentous achievement as the team had managed just one safety in its first eight games. But then Thorpe fumbled a bad snap. The ball was scooped up at the two-yard line by the Bears' George Halas, who scampered ninety-eight yards for a touchdown. Halas' run stood as a record for forty-nine years. "I could feel Thorpe breathing down my neck all the way," he said later.

Still, Oorang remains one of the most unusual teams in the history of professional football. Walter Lingo, the owner of the Oorang Dog Kennels in Larue, Ohio, organized the team, made up entirely of Native Americans. During the 1922 and 1923 seasons, Lingo had the team travel the country to advertise his kennel and to sell the Airedales he bred. The team won only three times, but Lingo didn't care. Pre-game and halftime were what he considered important; that was when he made the players and the the Airedale dogs perform. The dogs retrieved targets. The players danced and threw tomahawks and knives. One player, named Long Time Sleep, even wrestled a bear.

~

Duluth opened its inaugural season on August 31, 1923, in Athletic Park, a minor-league baseball stadium where Duluth's West End meets West Duluth, just beyond the current Wade Stadium's outfield walls. Some three thousand fans filled the wooden bleachers around the park's home plate or stood along the football grid's freshly chalked sidelines, which were almost literally in the shadows of the Duluth Missabe and Iron Range Railway ore docks.

The fans watched "one of the most powerful offenses seen this season," as the *Duluth News Tribune* described the Kelley-Duluth team the following morning. The Duluth eleven "played rings around the Akron club in the first half."

The teams exchanged punts through most of those first two quarters, Duluth gaining yardage with each exchange. Kenneth M. "Bunk" Harris handled the punting duties. A former standout at Duluth Central High School and Syracuse University, the six foot, 190-pound Harris had been born in Duluth in June 1894 and played six games for his hometown team in 1923.

The play that turned the game was a forward pass from Harris to Bill Rooney, a six-foot-two, 194-pound fullback, guard, halfback, and quarterback. Like his brothers Joe and Cobb Rooney, he had been a star for Roosevelt High School in Virginia, Minnesota. Although Rooney couldn't handle the pass, and the ball bounced off his hands, Duluth's Dicky O'Donnell stretched out his six-foot frame to haul it in.

A Duluth Denfeld product, O'Donnell was among the Twin Ports' shipyard workers who participated in a semi-pro league during World War I. Born in 1900 in Duluth, O'Donnell played seven games for Kelley-Duluth in 1923.

After snagging the deflected pass, he raced as fast as he could carry his 190-pound body before finally being caught and tackled at the Akron thirty-yard line.

Three line plunges and five yards later, Duluth's Harris heaved another pass, this one to Joe Rooney, who grabbed it and slid across the goal line. Sternaman drop kicked the extra point.

Before holding off a late Akron rally, Duluth wrapped up its scoring in the third quarter with a forty-yard drop kick by Sternaman (the hero of the next morning's headlines), bringing the Kelleys a 10-7 opening-day victory over Akron.

The "team started its initial league season in the right style," and the home crowd left Athletic Park "satisfied," the newspaper's Louis H. Gollop reported. The victory provided optimism for the season—and for Duluth's prospects in the NFL. "If Akron is an example of the average league team, Duluth fans can rest assured that they are going to see some classy football this season," Gollop wrote.

The new pro club was off in the right style, indeed.

～

For their second game, the Kelleys faced the Minneapolis Marines before about 2,500 fans at Minneapolis' Nicollet Park on October 8. Shortly after the start of the game, Sternaman fumbled and the Marines recovered on the Kelleys' twenty-five-yard line. "But the Minneapolis boys, boasting of several former college stars, couldn't gain an inch through the visitors' line," the *Duluth News Tribune* reported. A drop kick from thirty-three yards missed by inches and the Marines' opportunity was completely squandered.

Sternaman missed a pair of field goal attempts, the longest a thirty-five-yarder that sailed wide just before halftime. The first half ended scoreless for both teams.

Following intermission, the Kelleys had the ball at the Marines' forty-yard line. From there, Bunk Harris dropped back and then let loose with a rainbow pass that found Dicky O'Donnell at the Marines' fifteen-yard line. O'Donnell lumbered into the end zone untouched.

In the fourth quarter, a fumble recovered by the Kelleys led to a drop kick by Sternaman. Kelley-Duluth shut out the Marines of Minneapolis, 10-0.

The morning paper left little doubt about the enthusiasm of local fans. "Duluth Continues On Way To National Grid Title," the headline boasted. "Duluth held the upper hand most of the way by reason of the stonewall defense the line put up," the story said. The Marines' first quarter recovery of Sternaman's fumble was "the closest the Marines came to a touchdown all afternoon."

~

Back in Duluth at Athletic Park on October 21, the 2-0 Kelley-Duluth club faced the Hammond Pros. Sternaman, according to the next day's sports page, booted a "pretty" drop kick from the thirty-three-yard line early in the first quarter, giving the home team all the points it would need in a 3-0 victory.

"Duluth played like a championship team yesterday, and there is no getting away from that fact," Gollop wrote. He called Kelley-Duluth a "sweet football team. With the full recovery of Bunk Harris, Bill Rooney, Joe Rooney, Sternaman, and Gilbert, Duluth will continue its march toward the national championship."

~

Walter John "Wally" Gilbert emerged from that game a bona fide star. He "kept the fans on their toes with his punting," according to Gollop. "This baby sure did boot 'em high and far. It was a pleasure to watch him average about sixty yards on almost every punt, and once he booted the oval from his own five-yard line to back of the visiting goal posts. Some kick.... Not satisfied with punting his way to fame, Gilbert had to do a whole lot of line smashing."

Gilbert was an only child, born six days before Christmas in 1900 in Oscoda, Michigan. His family moved to Duluth when he was just four or five years old. He "grew up as a special sort of athlete," said his son, Minnesota sportswriter John Gilbert. "It wasn't destiny because his upbringing was spare and without sports connections. He simply excelled at every athletic endeavor he attempted."

At Duluth Denfeld High School, Gilbert was dominant on the football field, basketball court, and baseball diamond. His reputation as an athlete grew when he and a couple of buddies went to Valparaiso University in Indiana. He was a halfback on the football team, earning All-American honors his senior year. He was a guard and forward on the basketball team and a third baseman on the baseball team. His senior year he captained the football and baseball teams and possibly the basketball team.

"He was six foot one [and 180] pounds and had large, muscular hands and a quick, instinctive ability to read situations and hone his reactions," John Gilbert said of his father. "When he'd get a baseball glove, first thing he did was cut a hole out of the pocket. He wanted to feel the ball hit his hand so he could get rid of it quicker."

Gilbert played minor-league baseball before coming home and joining the Kelley-Duluth team. He was a champion curler, too, competing—and often winning—at the old Duluth Curling Club.

On October 27 the Kelleys had a rematch with the Minneapolis Marines in Duluth. The Duluth defensive line's first major challenge came just after the opening kickoff. Minneapolis blocked a punt and recovered the ball on the Kelleys' five-yard line. "But the good old line—every member of it—proved his worth," wrote Gollop. "Minneapolis lost the ball on downs with but a foot to go."

A few minutes later, a long pass put the Marines on the Kelleys' doorstep again. But again, Duluth held on four downs, the defensive line impenetrable. "When the ball was recovered, it is doubtful if more than a fraction of an inch separated Minneapolis from a touchdown," Gollop reported.

Gilbert scored a rushing touchdown and Sternaman added a drop kick in a 9-0 "licking." Kelley-Duluth improved to four wins against no losses in their inaugural NFL season.

"Try and stop us," Gollup wrote. "The Kelley-Duluth football team is headed for the national championship. Yes, try and stop us!"

The next game, on November 11, brought the Kelleys to Milwaukee to face the Milwaukee Badgers. After a scoreless opening half, the Duluth eleven grabbed the lead, thanks to a "series of line smashes and long end runs [that] put the ball on Milwaukee's 30-yard line," the newspaper reported. When a pair of inside running attempts gained little, Sternaman dropped back for a kick. "His effort [sailed] through the goal posts perfectly," the story said. Kelleys, 3-0.

Milwaukee answered immediately, however, moving the ball down the field with a combination of a "smashing line attack" and "several well-placed forward passes." A place kick by the Badgers tied the score at 3-3.

In the fourth quarter, both teams missed the uprights with drop-kick attempts.

With time running down, the Badgers hit a long pass, which set them up for a field goal attempt. The kick split the uprights, setting off euphoria in Brew City: "Thousands of fans rushed madly onto the field, and it was only after a long delay that several…blue coats were able to clear the field for the minute of action that remained," the *Duluth News Tribune* reported.

The 6-3 heartbreaker, their first loss, was bad enough, but the Kelleys suffered another blow in this one: Wally Gilbert was forced to watch the game from the sidelines after breaking three ribs.

~

Miraculously—and with lots of tape—the star of the Kelley-Duluth team, Wally Gilbert, returned to action the following week, broken ribs and all. He was able to play in his team's final two games of the season.

On November 18 in Chicago, the Cardinals started the game's scoring with a thirty-yard drop kick. "The Duluth team…put up a good fight," a Windy City sportswriter reported, but the Kelleys' reliance on running plays, or "straight football," proved a wrongheaded strategy. The Cardinals were able to keep the ball on their opponent's end of the field all day, and the Kelleys lost the game, 10-0.

The Chicago crowd didn't rush the field following the victory, and that was probably a good thing. Some 8,500 fans attended the game, the largest Sunday crowd for any professional game the entire season.

An estimated 3,000 fans turned out on a rainy, gray day in Green Bay the following week. The Packers—then wearing blue and gold uniforms modeled after Notre Dame—were led by future-legend Curly Lambeau.

The linemen for both teams proved unmovable in this one, and the game quickly became a passing contest. In the opening quarter, Sternaman had a forty-yard field goal attempt blocked. After a "wild and wooly air attack [that] chased the Packers way back into the Bays' back yard," the Kelleys' pass into the end zone fell incomplete.

Meanwhile, "with machine-line perfection, the Packers battered their way through the Minnesota champions," the Green Bay media reported. "There was little wasted energy. The big Bay Blues went to their business with a smashing, crashing offense that paved the way for victory. Green Bay had plenty of opposition. Duluth was in there battling for every inch of ground, but class tells in football, just as any place else, and the Packers were a good point better than their fire-eating opponents."

The Wisconsin fans cheered and hollered as their Packers were "polishing off" the Kelleys, 10-0, "in a corking good exhibition of pigskin chasing."

Green Bay's coverage continued, "'Little Joe' Sternaman didn't live up to advance notices. At least three of his teammates had it over the former Illinois star like a tent. [Dicky] O'Donnell played superb football at end. [Howard] 'Hot Dog' Kiley talked his way into every play at tackle, while [Bunk] Harris turned in a mighty job at fullback."

Howard Kiley was a five-foot-eight tackle and guard who was born in 1896 in Michigan. He played for Navy before joining the Kelleys for three seasons.

~

Dropping their last three contests, the Kelley-Duluths finished their inaugural NFL season with four wins and three losses. They were out of the hunt for the title, but their record was good enough for seventh place in the twenty-team league. More than respectable. The Duluth team outscored its opponents 35-33 with Bunk Harris leading the way in passing (he completed nine of twenty-eight attempts for 171 yards and no touchdowns) and Bill Rooney setting the pace in rushing with 31 yards. Harris gained 25 on the ground while Gilbert pounded his way to 20 yards and a touchdown.

The Canton Bulldogs went undefeated for a second straight season to claim a second straight championship, and it had not been easy. The Ohioans had to defeat top-notch teams three times on the road en route to their crown. They beat the Chicago Bears in Chicago 6-0 on two fourth-quarter field goals by Wilbur "Pete" Henry. Two weeks later, at Comiskey Park, they took on a Cardinals team that had come into the game with a five-win, zero-loss record, including a 60-0 shellacking of the Rochester Jeffersons. The Bulldogs' Lou Smythe, who'd become the only player in NFL history to lead the league in both rushing and passing touchdowns, provided the heroics and the Bulldogs prevailed 7-3. And two weeks after that, the Bulldogs knocked off the previously unbeaten Cleveland Indians, 46-10. The only blemish on their record was a 3-3 tie to the Buffalo All-Americans.

The Chicago Bears were again the runners-up with a record of nine wins, two losses, and one tie. The Green Bay Packers finished third at seven wins, two losses, and one tie. The Milwaukee Badgers took fourth place with seven wins, two losses, and three ties. And the Minneapolis Marines finished 1923 in thirteenth place with two wins, five losses, and two ties.

With one season under their belt, the Kelleys needed to capitalize on their relatively strong showing and get ready for the 1924 season. Luckily—and, as it would turn out, pivotally—a young volunteer, just in his mid-twenties, came forward and asked to become the team's secretary-treasurer. That was Ole Haugsrud, a native of Superior, Wisconsin, with a love of sports and a knack for scheduling, promoting, and managing a team.

Haugsrud had developed the organizational and promotional skills that would eventually serve him so well in the world of professional football years earlier, in high school. He'd been cut from the basketball team at Superior Central High School (where he'd go on to graduate in 1919), but had not been ready to give up the game. So Haugsrud, then nineteen, had organized an independent hardcourt team, the Red Devils. With players who, like him, had deemed unworthy to play for the varsity by Superior Central High Coach Ira Tubbs, Haugsrud had been arranging games in small towns all over North-western Wisconsin. In places like Iron River, Bayfield, and Washburn, Haug-srud's bunch played city teams and other independent squads, always hoping to attract enough spectators to make enough money to cover their train fare back home. Meanwhile, Tubbs and the Superior Central team went on to win the 1919 Wisconsin state championship.

Haugsrud sniffed a game he just had to book. "We knew those fellows on the team, and we were proud of them," Haugsrud explained. "But we weren't convinced they were better than we were."

He challenged the champs to a game. "There was a lot of razzing back and forth," he said. "They wouldn't go for it at first…. Coach Tubbs could see no reason for such a game; his team would have everything to lose and nothing to gain, so he told us. But we kept riding the ball players and told them they were scared to play us."

Finally, one of the varsity players, Ted Whereatt, no doubt fed up with the taunting, told Haugsrud he'd pay a visit. He brought along his teammates, but not Coach Tubbs, and agreed to play. Haugsrud and his band of rejects—

including Doc Kelly, Monk Johnson, and Ole Sorensen—humbled the state champions, 34-18.

The story of the game was big news, and Haugsrud knew it. He bolted straight to the offices of the *Superior Evening Telegram*, which was owned then by the family of Morgan Murphy, the manager of Superior Central's varsity team. The *Telegram* refused to run with the story.

"Apparently, they wanted no part of publishing something which would tarnish the high school team's reputation," Haugsrud later recalled. The *Telegram*'s sports editor "kicked me out of his office, saying he'd get fired if he ran such an item. 'Well,' I said, 'this is news and I'm going to get it printed.' So I got on a streetcar and came over to Duluth. [I] went up to the newsroom of the *Duluth News Tribune* and showed the article to the sportswriter there. He leaped out of his chair and exclaimed, 'This is a scoop! Can you prove this, Ole?' I assured him I could, and the Duluth paper came out with a story on Sunday morning—eight columns across the top of the sports page: 'Superior Red Devils Defeat Wisconsin State Champions.'

"We were famous overnight," Haugsrud recalled. "We had a hundred bookings the next season, sometimes two and three the same night, and we had to form several units of the team to meet the demand." Haugsrud would later joke that the Harlem Globetrotters had copied his Red Devils' multiple-team business strategy to maximize their own scheduling—and bottom line.

"We were just a bunch of high school kids, but we traveled around quite a bit and we kept the team going for several years," Haugsrud said.

The Red Devils, sometimes known as "Haugsrud's Wonders," barnstormed across Minnesota, Wisconsin, the Dakotas, and northern Iowa. When they were home in Superior they often hung around the corner of Ninth Street and Tower Avenue, where Bill Stein's Billiards Academy was located. The pool hall became a sort-of team headquarters.

Haugsrud played for the Red Devils, but devoted most of his attention to scheduling games, promoting his team, and arranging travel. He didn't realize he was in training for the NFL.

~

The man sports columnist Bruce Bennett would one day call "without a doubt, Duluth's finest and most beloved sportsman," that *Sports Illustrated* would refer to as a "mild-mannered little Swede," and that thousands of Minnesota Vikings fans would come to know as "Uncle Ole" had been born Oluf Haugsrud on May 13, 1899, the only child of Minnie and Helge Haugsrud. His father operated a wholesale produce business. The family attended church on Sundays at Concordia Lutheran in Superior. Even when he was young—and was still attending Superior Erickson Elementary and delivering 350 copies of the *Superior Evening Telegram* every afternoon—Haugsrud helped his father at work. He learned business savvy.

After graduating Superior Central, Haugsrud worked for Duluth Paper and Specialties, and he became a seaman, working as a fireman and an oiler on the Great Lakes and beyond. His ships took him to the West Indies three times and to South America once. Returning home, he enrolled at Superior Normal School, now the University of Wisconsin-Superior. But he spent less than a year in college classrooms. His father died, and he decided to return home to run the wholesale produce business. But his love of sports drew him to the Kelley-Duluth team.

The Kelleys would need someone like Haugsrud for the bumpy road ahead. And a new volunteer secretary-treasurer was far from the only addition—or change—as the Kelley-Duluth football franchise prepared for the 1924 NFL campaign.

TWO

SOPHOMORE
SEASON

The Kelleys faced growing financial woes as the franchise headed into 1924, largely because Duluth lacked "anything like a modern stadium," according to new secretary-treasurer Haugsrud. "Seating arrangements [at Duluth's Athletic Park] were inadequate, and at many of the games even the women patrons had to stand. The fans were loyal to a grand degree, but after all there was a limit to the amount of punishment they should be called upon to take."

Haugsrud didn't mention what the bathroom facilities were like—or if there were any. Sportswriter and broadcasting legend Halsey Hall reported once that there were no locker rooms at the park and that the playing field was an "uneven, coal-dust surface." The dust was more likely iron dust, given the proximity of the field to the ore docks.

The bottom line was that not enough fans were enduring the punishment to regularly attend games and the Kelleys were hemorrhaging money. So much money that team founder Marshall C. Gebert, fed up with the situation, abandoned his position as team coach. Fellow founder Dewey Scanlon took over, adding coach to his already demanding dual role of player and team manager.

Scanlon was one of nine returning Kelleys players in 1924, the others being Wally Gilbert, Art "The Swede" Johnson, Howard Kiley, Allen MacDonald, Russ Method, Bill and Joe Rooney, Bill Stein, and Doc Williams.

The team roster's toughest casualty had to be its quarterback and team leader Joey Sternaman. He had actually left at the end of the previous season when it became obvious the Kelleys weren't going to be able to schedule any more games. Unusual league rules allowed him to return to his former team, the Chicago Bears, without any compensation to the Kelley-Duluth franchise. Sternaman was part of Chicago's run at the league championship for their final four games of 1923 and then remained in the Windy City, not only for the 1924 campaign, but until his playing days ended in 1930 at the age of 30.

Also gone from the Kelleys' 1923 roster was Dicky O'Donnell, who was picked up by the Green Bay Packers in the off-season. The Minneapolis Marines nabbed John Madigan of Madison Lake, Minnesota. Madigan had played college football in the Gopher State for the University of St. Thomas.

Other players left because of injuries or because they'd had enough or because they wanted—or needed—to work "regular" jobs that paid better and that could support families. Roddy Dunn, a Duluth Denfeld product, hung up his spikes after only two games in 1923. Ira Haaven of McIntosh, Minnesota, and a Hamline University graduate, left football after a three-game pro career. And Bunk Harris of Duluth Central and Syracuse University quit after playing just six games for the Kelleys in 1923.

Ten new athletes rounded out the 1924 roster, including twenty-four-year-old Cobb Rooney of Virginia, Minnesota, the younger brother of Joe and Bill. Other new players included Eugene "Oke" or "Curly" Carlson, a Two Harbors native and a "giant lineman from Iowa State University," as Haugsrud described him; Herbert W. Clow, an undersized end at five foot, four inches tall and 180 pounds who played for Duluth Central and for the University of Wisconsin-Superior; Arthur Edward "Art" or "George" Engstrom, a five-foot-nine, 185-pound guard and tackle from Knox, Indiana; Doc Kelly, a fullback and halfback originally from Chicago; William "Bill" O'Toole, a twenty-four-year-old guard; James Leo "Jim" Sanford, a tackle from Brooklyn, New York, and a product of Lehigh University; Lief Richard Strand, a center from Two Harbors; Jack Underwood of Hinckley, Minnesota, and of Duluth Central High School; and Roy L. Vexall, a twenty-two-year-old, 190-pound end and fullback from Minnesota.

In all, nineteen names filled the Kelleys' 1924 roster. But there was still the franchise's financial situation. "The league was far flung back then," Haugsrud remembered. "We traveled by train and not jetliner. Each team scheduled its own games, which made it possible to avoid long jumps and thus save money. The league was still in a more or less secure state financially and the officials deemed it best for the team owners to kind of feel their way around."

The Kelley-Duluth franchise felt their way around to a surprising solution to their money trouble. The players paid to play, essentially taking over and running the team like a co-op. By contributing up to thirty dollars apiece toward expenses, the players expected to get a share of the team's profits through gate receipts—at least when there were gate receipts and profits, which wasn't as often as they hoped.

~

Money was tight for all the teams in those early years, but especially for the ones from smaller towns like Duluth or Canton or Rock Island. As a result, teams tended to come and go, resulting in frequent changes within the league.

In January 1924 the NFL granted a franchise to Kansas City, Missouri: the Blues. At the league meeting the following June, Frankford (a section of Philadelphia) was granted entrance for the Yellow Jackets. At the same meeting, St. Louis' All-Stars team was canceled, and Buffalo transferred owners and adopted a new name, switching from the All-Americans to the Bisons. The Oorang Indians were given permission to suspend operations for a year, but the time requested to reorganize didn't help—the team never reformed. And the league ordered the struggling Toledo Maroons to transfer to a new city or suspend operations. It moved to Kenosha, Wisconsin, where it would play only one forgettable season, finishing with just two wins against seven losses.

After the meeting, the Louisville Brecks suspended operations, but didn't completely dissolve. The club from Kentucky continued to send representatives to meetings and other league functions.

On August 3, Sam Deutsch, the Cleveland sports promoter who owned the Cleveland Indians, purchased the Canton Bulldogs for $2,500. The Bulldogs had won two straight championships, but not even success could guarantee solvency. High salaries, increasing travel expenses, and a small, outdated stadium combined to leave the franchise spiraling out of financial control. Deutsch decided to deactivate Canton in 1924 while inviting its ten best players to join his Cleveland team, which became the Cleveland Bulldogs. Seven of them did, which paid off handsomely for Deutsch.

The 1924 season opened with twenty franchises, but just eighteen fielded teams.

~

The revamped Kelley-Duluth team faced Curly Lambeau and the Green Bay Packers in their season opener, with an estimated three thousand fans pouring into Athletic Park in West Duluth on the bright, crisp afternoon of September 28, 1924. The Packers were the NFL's preseason favorites; their lineup was loaded with "gridiron stars selected from several points in the east and the west," as the *Duluth News Tribune* reported. The Duluth eleven was given only a small chance to hold its own in the game.

Referee Halsey Hall, later the voice of the Minnesota Twins, put the ball in play. The opening half was filled with booming punts and with both teams content to play for field position. The strategy carried into the third quarter before a break gave the Packers their first opportunity.

Doc Kelly, a dentist in Superior who would become known as the "Old Tooth Carpenter" to his teammates, was playing in his first game for the Kelleys and was playing well, his punts pinning back the Green Bay squad again and again. But on this punt attempt, the Packers broke through the line and pressured Kelly. He got his kick off, but just barely. The five-foot-ten, 170-pound graduate of Superior Central High School and Northwestern University shanked the boot, the ball careening out of bounds at his team's own thirty-one-yard line.

The Packers went right to work. A series of line plunges took the ball to the fifteen. A run off right tackle gained four more yards. A sweep to the left picked up another four and then a return to the right gained enough for a first down.

Lambeau fumbled on the next play, but a teammate got on top of the ball. The Packers' "Cub" Buck then faked a drop kick, giving the ball instead to Lambeau. Duluth wasn't fooled. The Kelleys vaunted defensive line smothered Lambeau for a two-yard loss.

Buck's next drop kick attempt was no fake. It split the uprights, giving Green Bay a 3-0 lead.

"The large gallery of Duluth fans felt a sickening feeling creep over their mid-sections," the Duluth paper would report the following morning. "But it was soon passed, for the Kelleys seemed to take the three points which were scored against them as the needed tonic."

Bill Rooney offered the partisan crowd a reason for hope when he returned the ensuing kickoff twenty yards. After a five-yard holding penalty against the Kelleys and a five-yard run by Doc Kelly, Duluth got off a beauty of a punt—a fifty-five-yarder to the Green Bay twenty-five.

On the next play, Doc Williams broke through the line, pounding Lambeau two yards into his own backfield. He hit the Green Bay legend so hard, the ball squirted free. Kelly fell on it for the Kelleys.

Back on offense, Duluth's Bill Rooney plowed ahead for three yards, and Kelly, off the right side, gained five more. Then Cobb Rooney "executed a neat bit of strategy which took the Packers completely off their guard," the paper wrote. He tossed a short pass, near the sidelines, to John Patrick 'Jack' Underwood, another new member of the Duluth club. The six foot, two-hundred-pound, twenty-seven-year-old end took what today would be called a "screen pass." He slipped by one tackler, shook off Lambeau, and then struggled over the goal line before being downed. Duluth was ahead 6-3. Despite an off-the-mark pass attempt for the extra point, the home crowd went nuts.

Duluth's missed extra point seemed to set a precedent for the team. As the clock ran down, the Kelleys missed two drop kicks. Joe Rooney dropped one pass and let another sail through his outstretched arms, both near the end zone. Bill Stein got a fifty-yard penalty for "slugging," and there was also a five-yard penalty against the Kelleys for stalling, both helping a last-minute rally by the Packers—which still came up short.

The Kelleys were 1-0 in the win-loss columns. It was a big win against the favored team, and a bit of revenge for the previous season.

~

Steady rains left the field at Athletic Park a muddy mess on October 5 as the Kelleys prepared to do battle with the Minneapolis Marines for their second game of the season.

Kelleys' Coach Dewey Scanlon came up with a brilliant strategy to neutralize the horrible playing conditions, however. He rotated two three-man backfields, one trio featuring Wally Gilbert, Bill Rooney, and Russell G. "Cuss" Method, a Duluth Denfeld graduate and "one of the greatest backs ever developed in the Northwest," as *Duluth News Tribune* sportswriter Bruce Bennett once wrote.

Rooney made his trio's best play in the game, taking a punt at his own twenty-yard line, from where he "dodged and twisted away from several tacklers and then squirmed and zig-zagged down the field for thirty-three yards," as the *News Tribune*'s Cubby Campbell reported.

The other trio was made up of Doc Kelly, Allen J. MacDonald, and Roy L. Vexall.

In the opening quarter, Vexall started a rally by returning a punt fifteen yards to the Kelleys' forty-two-yard line. He, Kelly, and MacDonald then took turns with the ball. They "smashed their way through the Marine defense," Campbell wrote. As the first quarter came to an end, they had reached the Marines' twenty-yard line.

Gilbert went in for the kick. "The former Valparaiso star wiped the mud from his hands and shoes and with a deliberateness that was almost exasperating," Campbell wrote. "He booted the pigskin through the uprights of the Marines' goal." 3-0, Duluth.

As the game continued, three Minneapolis runners occasionally broke into open territory and shook off tacklers, but "the work of the Duluth line was good time and again," Campbell wrote. "The forwards would break through and throw the Marines back for losses. Once, when the Marines had the ball in the middle of the field, the Duluth line spilled three consecutive plays for losses.

"Had the field been dry, it is probable that a far more wonderful football game would have been witnessed," he wrote.

But a win is a win, even if ugly. To the delight of more than three thousand Duluth fans, three points were all the Kelleys needed. And 2-0 was a good start for the season.

~

The third game of 1924 campaign came three weeks later, on October 26. Duluth faced the Kenosha, Wisconsin, Maroons, a team with an all-star reputation.

The Duluth defense scored first when Lief Strand tackled Kenosha tailback Dick Vick in the Maroons' own end zone for a two-point safety. Later in the first quarter, Wally Gilbert intercepted a Maroons' pass and tore down the field. Shaking off tackler after tackler, Gilbert wasn't pulled down until he reached the Maroons' three-yard line. The Kelleys called Gilbert's number for two straight plays, but he was unable to finish the deal, his line plunges coming up short both times. On the next play, Cuss Method went around the left end and stiff-armed three different Maroons to literally punch home Duluth's second score. Gilbert tacked on the extra point for a 9-0 lead.

He would use his foot again for a field goal with just two minutes left in the second quarter. The half ended with Kelley-Duluth up 12-0.

The second half featured the Rooney brothers. Bill and Cobb teamed up for a touchdown pass (Bill to Cobb) to make it 18-0, and the route was on. Gilbert's extra point attempt failed. Joe Rooney would get his glory later.

The Duluth team dominated again in the fourth quarter. Gilbert intercepted yet another pass by charging between two Kenosha receivers and leaping high. He side-stepped players and tore down the sidelines for sixty-five yards. No one caught him this time, and he got his touchdown—as well as the extra point. Duluth went up 25-0.

In the fourth quarter Joe Rooney wasn't about to let his brothers have all the fun. He picked off another Maroons' pass and raced thirty-five yards to the end zone. Once again Wally Gilbert added the extra point. When the final gun sounded, the scoreboard stood at 32-0.

Throughout the game, the Kelleys continued to rotate backfield trios. All six runners were able to remain fresh, which allowed them to punish the Maroons' defense. The Duluth team's offensive and defensive lines starred in this game, too. Kenosha failed to gain a single first down on the ground and only four through the air. The defensive line was anchored that day by Howard Kiley, Doc Williams, and Joe Rooney. The offensive line was held down by Art "The Swede" Johnson, Bill Stein, and Jack Underwood. Lief Strand delivered punishment from both sides of the line, and made the safety in the first-quarter. But with three touchdowns off interceptions, the defensive backfield did the most to put points on the board.

With the victory, Duluth improved to 3-0 on the season, already the only undefeated team. Optimism, obviously, was cresting, just as it had during a winning streak a year earlier. The most praise for the lopsided victory went to Gilbert. His thirty-five-yard scamper off right tackle was considered the play of a game filled with great plays, even though he didn't score. "It seemed that every man on the Kenosha eleven dove for Gilbert and missed him," the *News Tribune* reported. "His run was one of the most brilliant features of the game."

The Duluth crowd was "frantic with glee" throughout the game, the hometown newspaper said. But of course the home-based media would write something positive like that. Sportswriters covering the earliest days of the National Football League made little effort to hide their love of the home team or to even give the impression of impartiality. Opposing teams, it seemed, were always boastful mountains for the hometown heroes to conquer. And the good guys always seemed to be on the verge of a championship.

The colorful story written about the Kelleys' triumph over the Maroons was a good example:

Bewildering their opponents with an intricate and varied offensive attack, and at the same time presenting a forward and secondary defense line which smashed every attempt of the invaders to batter their way beyond the middle of the field, the Kelley-Duluth football eleven rose to glorious heights Sunday afternoon when it crushed the highly touted Nash-Simmons Maroons....

The mighty Duluth team remains at the top of the United States Professional Football league today and rates as the most probable winner of the championship as a result of its victories over three powerful 'pro' elevens.

Physical perfection, coupled with marvelous team play, caused the downfall of the purported all-star aggregation from Kenosha.

Balked at every turn, the Maroons presented a sorry sight when in the final quarter Duluth's secondary backfield went into the battle and literally ripped the Kenosha eleven to ribbons.

For three quarters they had been battered and shunted up and down the field unmercifully, and when the reserves rushed into the game, they had neither the morale [nor the] stamina to stop the terrific onslaught which netted the fourth and final touchdown of the game.

At no time in the history of professional football at the Head of the Lakes did a gridiron eleven ever work with such perfect unison and harmony as the Kelleys did Sunday in squashing the reputations of the Nash-Simmons aggregation.

~

Fanaticism for the undefeated Kelleys was understandable on November 2, 1924, when the team arrived in Minneapolis for a rematch with the Marines.

The game was "bitterly fought," according to news coverage. That was especially true in the first half when the closest either team came to scoring was a missed drop kick from twenty-five yards by the Kelleys' Wally Gilbert. The Marines' aerial attack was effective in the early going, but Duluth broke up passes at key moments.

After intermission, the Kelleys intercepted a pass deep in Marines' territory. Given an opportunity, Cobb Rooney and Gilbert went to work, smashing through the defensive line for hard-fought chunks of real estate. They pushed the ball to the Marines' six-yard line. From there, Cobb threw into the end zone and hit Jack Underwood. The twenty-seven-year-old, six foot, two-hundred-pound Underwood staked the Kelleys to a 6-0 lead as the point-after kick flew wide.

Duluth nearly scored again late in the game, launching what was becoming a trademark, end-of-game, time-running-down aerial onslaught. The offensive was led by Rooney, Gilbert, and MacDonald. The Kelleys advanced the ball to the Marines' six-yard line, but then turned it over on downs.

Didn't matter—thanks to the Kelleys' defense, led by linemen Howard Kiley, Doc Williams, and others, the Duluth team was able to hold on for the 6-0 victory.

And a 4-0 win-loss season record.

Imagine the optimism—and fanaticism—then.

∽

The fifth game for Duluth gave the team a rematch with Curly Lambeau and the Packers on November 9 in Green Bay.

The Packers struck first. With a few minutes left in the first quarter, Lambeau hurled a touchdown pass from the Kelleys' fifteen-yard line. Then just before the end of the first half, Lambeau connected again, and at halftime the score was 13-0, the Packers having missed one extra point attempt.

In the third quarter, using a mix of line-plunging runs and short passes, Duluth worked the ball to the Green Bay thirty-three-yard line. But a fumble there on a fake drop kick gave the ball right back to the Packers. It was the only time Duluth threatened the end zone. During the second half, Duluth held Green Bay from scoring, but the Packers already had what they needed to avenge their earlier season loss. The final score remained at 13-0.

Duluth's passing in this game was described by one sportswriter as "miserable." Lambeau, meanwhile, was brilliant. He picked up chunks of yards on the ground, plunging into the center of the line and around end, and led the Packers' "bewildering air attack."

The Kelleys dropped to 4-1 on the season, but didn't drop from their perch atop the league standings.

∽

The ball was next put into play November 23 in Rock Island, Illinois, against the Rock Island Independents.

Gilbert once again was the star. He displayed "expert forward passing, kicking and open-field running" and was "the outstanding feature of the game," as an Illinois sportswriter gushed.

Gilbert "hurled a beautiful pass to big Bill Rooney who made a sensational run for a touchdown after shaking off three [would-be] tacklers." And he booted a drop kick from near the sidelines which was called "one of the most thrilling place kicks ever completed on a Rock Island gridiron." It sailed "squarely between the uprights." Although it was reported at the time to have been kicked from the Rock Island forty, some would later claim this kick sailed sixty yards through the uprights. Regardless, Gilbert accounted for all the scoring in the 9-0 win.

Reportedly, this game also was the one in which Gilbert took a snap near his own end zone, turned sideways and boomed a quick-kick punt that didn't come to rest until it reached the Independents' two-yard line. The Independents' star, Jim Thorpe, commented later, "I thought I'd have to chase it to the Mississippi."

In addition to a "flashing aerial attack," the Kelleys' defense, led by linemen Bill Stein and Doc Williams, was stifling. The Independents had only three first downs the entire game. Thorpe, the greatest player of his time, was "held helpless by the charging Duluth linemen. The northerners broke through Rock Island's forward wall time and again to spill the famous [Thorpe] for losses."

~

With five wins against only one loss, the Kelleys retained their spot atop the league standings, tied with the Cleveland Bulldogs. But a championship, like financial security, would elude the Duluth crew in 1924. Those first six games were all the games the Kelleys were able to schedule for the season. Despite beating the Green Bay Packers at home in the opener and then stuffing the great Jim Thorpe on the road to close out the season, Duluth finished in fourth place in the eighteen-team league.

Doc Williams, who played key roles in all five of the victories—including the hit on Curly Lambeau behind the line of scrimmage that forced a fumble in the opener, leading to the Kelleys' victory—was named to the 1924 All-Pro team.

Right behind the Kelleys in the standings was Rock Island, a team that had started strong behind the rejuvenated play of Jim Thorpe. The Independents shut out their first four opponents, but then lost 23-7 to the Kansas City Blues. Of course, they played that loss without their star tackle, Fred "Duke" Slater; Kansas City wouldn't allow a black player in the game. After losing to the Kelleys late in the season, Rock Island finished with six wins, two losses, and two ties.

The battle for the 1924 NFL championship came down to three teams: the Cleveland Bulldogs, Chicago Bears, and Frankford Yellow Jackets.

Frankford lost two games early on, but then an odd Philadelphia city law allowed the Yellow Jackets to rack up victories the rest of the way. The city ordinance prohibited spectator sports on Sundays, so the Yellow Jackets played home games on Saturdays and away games on Sundays. The double scheduling led to eleven victories against only two losses and a tie. Frankford wound up playing more than twice as many games as the Kelleys.

The Bears opened the season with a scoreless tie with Rock Island and a loss to Cleveland. But then Chicago didn't lose again, finishing at six wins, one loss, and four ties.

Cleveland beat the Bears in its opener and then finished the season with seven wins, one loss, and one tie. Both Bulldogs' blemishes came against Frankford.

Cleveland seemingly won the championship but then it scheduled an extra, late-season game against the runner-up Bears. The Bears won 23-0 and claimed the title. Player-coach George Halas insisted both teams had agreed that the game would decide the champion. When the Bulldogs didn't concede, the issue had to be resolved at the league meetings in January. League President Joe Carr said clubs didn't have the right to schedule games after November 30 without league permission. That meant that technically, according to the league, the Cleveland-Chicago finale had been an exhibition game. He ruled Cleveland finished in first place with Chicago second and Frankford third.

THREE

No Money, No Champions

Although the 1925 season would prove remarkable—in some ways—for the NFL, times continued to be tough financially with profits rare. That was especially true for small-city clubs.

The Kenosha Maroons and Racine Legion weren't able to field teams at all in 1925 and both forfeited their franchises. The Minneapolis Marines, which had won only three games while losing fourteen and tying twice in three seasons, were given league permission to suspend operations for the year. (They wouldn't reorganize again until 1929, and then as the Minneapolis Red Jackets. That Twin Cities team survived only two seasons, each as forgettable as any they had played as the Marines. The Red Jackets won only twice while losing a morale-numbing sixteen times and tying once.)

While three teams had left the NFL, five new teams joined: The Detroit Panthers, featuring owner, coach, and tailback Jimmy Conzelman; the Providence Steam Roller; a new Canton Bulldogs team, restarted after Sam Deutsch sold back the franchise after a year of inactivity to the Canton Professional Football Company; a new New York Giants; and the Pottsville Maroons, which had been, for two years, a powerhouse of an independent professional team. The league now stood at twenty teams.

The Kelley-Duluth franchise, whose players now had a unique and unusual cooperative ownership arrangement, faced a particularly difficult uphill battle against costs. Few teams were eager to, or could afford to, travel to Duluth, the league's northernmost outpost. The Kelleys "literally had to bribe opponents to book games with them," according to author Ross Bernstein.

And if that wasn't bad enough, Haugsrud recalled that "[Duluth had] one of those cold, rainy autumns, [so] the fans decided to remain at home.... It's possible we could have [made] some profit on the home games that fall if weather conditions had not gone against us. We had a pretty good team, but no money." The Kelleys' player-owners were forced to dig deep to cover expenses, sometimes coughing up as much as $44 each per game.

That had to be an especially difficult shock for new players like Charles Terrence "Charlie" Black, a twenty-four-year-old, five-foot-nine, 160-pound end from Alton, Illinois. He played for Kansas University before arriving in Duluth. Also new were Fred "Gibby" Denfield, a Duluth Central graduate and an All-American guard and tackle for Navy; Michael "Mike" Koziak, a thirty-three-year-old guard; John "Mickey" McDonnell, a star from Duluth Cathedral High School; Richard Wallace "Wally" O'Neill, a six foot, twenty-six-year-old end, guard, and tackle who had also played for Duluth Cathedral before suiting up for the University of Wisconsin-Superior and the University of Michigan; and Jimmy E. "Rex" Tobin, a twenty-six-year-old end.

Robert "Rube" Marshall, Duluth's first black player, also joined the Kelleys in 1925. He had last suited up in 1921 for the Rock Island Independents, playing seven games in Illinois. When the American Professional Football Association had formed in 1920, Marshall was already playing for the Independents, and Fritz Pollard for the Akron Pros; they became the first two African-Americans in the league. Marshall joined the Kelley-Duluth team at age forty-five, one of only six players in NFL history forty-five or older. Tall and wide at six foot two and 195 pounds, Marshall had been born in Milwaukee but went to high school in Minneapolis. He had gone on to become a collegiate star in baseball, track, hockey, boxing, and football, earning All-American honors for the University of Minnesota football team. The Gophers won twenty-seven games with Marshall at end between 1904 and 1906. They lost only twice and outscored their opponents 1,283 to 63. In one 1906 game, Marshall kicked a game-winning field goal from sixty yards.

The Kelleys' continuing financial woes could be blamed for at least some of the departures from the 1924 Duluth roster. Gone were a quartet of players who had suited up for just one game each: Herb Clow of Duluth, Art Engstrom of Indiana, Jim Sanford of Brooklyn, and Bill O'Toole.

Lief Strand ended his pro career after just six games with the Kelley-Duluths in 1924; Roy Vexall hung up his spikes after only two games the previous year; and Allen MacDonald had walked away after two seasons. Joe Rooney left his brothers in Duluth to play with the Rock Island Independents.

~

But all was not lost for Duluth football fans as they streamed into Athletic Park for their team's third season opener against the renamed Kansas City Cowboys (formerly the Blues) on September 27, 1925. The Kelleys had a solid nucleus of returning veterans, including Wally Gilbert, Art Johnson, Howard Kiley, Russ Method, the remaining Rooney brothers Bill and Cobb, Bill Stein, and Doc Williams. And the Kelleys' fans had learned to count on a few things when spending autumn afternoons at Athletic Park. They knew to "go" before leaving home because the bathroom facilities were questionable, at best. They knew they'd likely spend the afternoon on their feet because the minor league baseball stadium's two thousand or so seats were uncomfortably hard and were well away from where the football field was laid out.

And they knew they were likely to see a home-team victory. To that point of the 1920s, not a single professional football eleven from Duluth had lost a home game.

Not long after the opening kickoff of their 1925 season, the Kelleys' first forward pass was intercepted and returned to midfield by the Cowboys. After three line plunges failed to net a first down, the Cowboys booted a place kick from fifty yards that sailed true, giving them an early 3-0 margin.

Later in the first quarter, Kansas City muffed a punt that Jack Underwood scooped up. The two-hundred-pound veteran lumbered down field with only two Cowboys to beat. He slipped past one of them but was pulled down at the twenty-five by the other. After three pass attempts missed their marks, Cuss Method dropped back for a field goal attempt. The charging Cowboys broke through the line, however, and blocked his kick.

In the second quarter, hard-playing Bill Stein recovered a fumbled punt for the Kelleys. A pass and a plunge by Method moved the ball once again to the Kansas City twenty-five-yard line. This time it was Wally O'Neill who was called upon to attempt the placekick. He got it off, but it sailed wide.

On their next possession, the Kelleys moved the ball once again, this time to the Kansas City thirty-five-yard line. The big gainer was a thirty-yard pass to Mickey McDonnell. But the Kelleys then misfired on three straight pass attempts that had to leave Coach Dewey Scanlon concerned about his team's aerial abilities. The ball went over on downs.

In the third quarter, Duluth had found a soft spot in the left side of the Kansas City line and ran at it repeatedly. Ecstatic fans roared louder with each gain. Cobb Rooney over right tackle. Doc Kelly plunging through the right side. The Kelleys marched the ball to their opponents' ten-yard line. But then, inexplicably, Duluth attempted an end run. It was stuffed. When a line plunge came up an agonizing few inches short of the goal line, the ball went over one more time on downs.

Later the Kelleys again drove into Cowboys' territory, only to be stopped by an interception. When the final gun sounded, Kansas City had the ball at midfield and were still in the lead at 3-0. One of only two victories for the Cowboys that entire season was secured.

The Duluth crowd filed out amid "perfect weather conditions [that had] brought out a colorful throng of fans who were treated with thrilling and spectacular feats throughout the contest," as the *Duluth News Tribune*'s Cubby Campbell reported. But those spectacular feats hadn't been enough to keep up the winning streak in Athletic Park.

～

Two weeks later, a crowd estimated at four thousand strong—the "largest football crowd in several seasons, brightly colored with feminine attire," according to the *Duluth News Tribune*—filled Athletic Park for the Kelleys' November 11 game against the Rock Island Independents.

After a scoreless first quarter, the Independents connected in the second quarter with a two-yard pass into the Kelleys' end zone. Duluth fans watched in stunned horror—the previous week the Kelleys had lost their first home game in years by a single field goal, and now here was an opponent's first touchdown at the park in several seasons. The home team trailed 0-6.

Moments later the Kelleys' Bill Stein lateraled poorly, allowing the ball to bounce away from teammate Wally Gilbert. Former Duluth player Joe Rooney pounced on it, giving the ball back to the Independents. After two runs and a first down, the visitors hit on another pass, five yards out from the end zone. The Kelleys' Cuss Method immediately tackled the receiver, driving him back and away from the end zone. The official ruled that the ball had been caught just across the goal line, putting the game at 0-12. Method and the other Kelleys protested, but the score stood.

A bright spot for Duluth came late in the game courtesy of Mickey Mc-Donnell, a "great little halfback" and, at one time, the lightest man in pro football, according to Ole Haugsrud.

"Less than half the size of most of his opponents," the *News Tribune* reported the following day. "[He] dashed wildly through the opposition in four thrilling sprints," earning himself a new nickname: "Pretty Mickey." His longest runs were twenty-five and forty-five yards. During one, "he sidestepped, twisted, and turned out of the reaching arms of tackler after tackler."

McDonnell also had a memorable punt return. He allowed the ball to bounce toward the goal line, assuming, or hoping, it would go into the end zone for a touch back. When he realized it wouldn't, he suddenly scooped it up and took off. "He slipped by three tacklers…and, getting into the open, shook off one opponent after another, finally being crunched to the ground on his 45-yard line under two beefy bodies which crashed into him from two sides," the newspaper reported.

The Kelleys' Wally Gilbert also had a "brilliant run" after a fake forward pass, a play McDonnell had used for a big gainer earlier in the game.

But it wasn't enough. Not even close. The Kelleys lost 0-12, with plenty of ugly play to mar an otherwise gorgeous day. Duluth completed only one pass the entire game, Wally Gilbert to Cuss Method. It gained a half yard. And time and again, Duluth's offensive line allowed the Independents' rushers to break through and put pressure on the passer—even when the passer was just trying to hand off the ball.

∽

The Kelleys' third game was played in a snowstorm at Comiskey Park in Chicago, home of baseball's White Sox.

A sloppy affair, Duluth took the lead in the second quarter after Cobb Rooney ran over center for five tough yards and then over guard for five more. Gilbert dropped back and launched a thirty-five-yard strike to "Pretty Mickey" McDonnell, who raced the final fifteen yards to the end zone. Gilbert's try for the point after was blocked, and the Kelleys took their 6-0 lead into halftime.

The Cardinals finally answered late in the third quarter on a twenty-yard touchdown pass. The game was tied 6-6, when in the fourth quarter the Cardinals won the game with a thirty-three-yard place kick. Another heart breaker for the Duluth eleven.

∽

Due to scheduling difficulties and continuing financial trouble, that third game would be the Kelleys' final game of 1925. At the end of this brief campaign, the team, in a nod to the bottom line, said good-bye to one of its more colorful players. The franchise sold lineman Howard Kiley to the Chicago Cardinals. Kiley "did furnish a lot of amusement" in his three seasons with Duluth, Haugsrud wrote.

> He and Art Juntilla, a middle-weight fighter who boxed under the name "Young Sharkey" and who played next to Kiley in the line, indulged in verbal fireworks before, during, and after every game. Kiley always insisted that Juntilla wasn't as dumb as an ox, but he wasn't any smarter, either.

> One day in the line, Kiley looked at Juntilla and said, "Your face would make a good blueprint for an idiot."

> And Juntilla came right back with, "I've seen better looking pans than yours under ice boxes. Your folks told me that when you were born, you were so homely they went into mourning."

The Duluth players often washed up after games and practices at the McKay Hotel, which was at 430 West First Street (where the *Duluth News Tribune* building now stands). Across First Street from the hotel—where Duluth's City Hall was later built—was a gas-lit field where the team held practices. The hotel—a brick building adorned with awnings over the sidewalks and illuminated by gas-powered lamps—served as clubhouse, training quarters, and dressing room. In the same building was a drug store and Turkish baths. The McKay's lodge-like lobby was filled with pillars and wooden rocking chairs and was dominated by a grand brick fireplace as well as the mounted trophies of moose, deer, and other north woods game.

Haugsrud recalled a time when Juntilla had had enough:

> Juntilla was getting peeved from all this ribbing. The blow-off came one evening…while the boys were taking their showers.

> The manager passed around the program for the next game. Juntilla saw the initials "C.H." before his name and inquired why.

> "They stand for Cement Head," roared Kiley.

> Juntilla swung at Kiley and chased him up to the old post office and federal building that stood at the corner of First Street and Fifth Avenue

[West]. Now remember, they were just in the locker room, [and] both boys were naked. Kiley hid in some shrubbery and Juntilla returned [to the locker room]. Later, one of the [other] players took a robe and slippers up to Kiley's hiding place, making it safe for him to walk down the avenue.

Another time, Kiley was incensed about how he was portrayed in a Duluth *Herald* story by Hemlock Peterson. "I'm going down to the *Herald* office [to] erase the sports department," he roared to Haugsrud, who remembered,

Kiley called up Sandy MacDonald, the sports editor, to prepare him for the invasion and announced what he was going to do to Hemlock. Seems that MacDonald was the only sportswriter on the *Herald* at that time, [but] the publisher insisted on all sports stories carrying bylines. So while MacDonald really wrote [about] football, he ghosted through Peterson rather than have his own name appear more than once on the page.

"Well, Hemlock is right here, and I'll have him stay until you arrive," MacDonald told Kiley over the phone.

"What kind of guy is he?" Kiley wanted to know.

"Just a big, agile fellow who love[s] to battle better than a baby likes pop. I'm sure you'll cheer him up with a challenge," MacDonald said. "His home's in Split Rock. They used him up there for skidding logs when the work got too heavy for the horses. He shaves with a blow torch and picks his teeth with a Bowie knife. He says for you to bring your wings with you, for when he finishes fanning the hilltops with you he'll toss you so high it will take you two hours to glide back to Earth. Hurry along, bruiser."

Kiley, I'm told, never visited the *Herald* office. Imagine that, a sportswriter scaring off a football player.

"We all liked Kiley," Haugsrud continued. "He was amazing in a rough sort of way and a good-hearted cuss." And even though he had been sold to Chicago and would never again be part of the team, Duluth hadn't heard the last of Howard Kiley.

~

Although the Kelleys weren't able to schedule additional games, the 1925 season rolled on for the rest of the NFL, and the race for the championship proved one wild ride—a raucous affair with a shocker of a finish. Because of the controversy a year earlier over which late-season games counted in the standings, the NFL extended the season to December 6. By then, the league assumed, all teams would have had ample time to schedule and complete the minimum eight games required to be considered for the championship. At that point, teams enduring a poor season could call it quits, while other teams could schedule additional games—and earn additional gate receipts—until December 20. But the league set itself up for more trouble, by allowing those extra games through the twentieth to count in the standings.

On December 6, the NFL's top two teams were the Chicago Cardinals, with a record of nine wins, one loss, and one tie, and the Pottsville Maroons at nine wins and two losses.

The Maroons and Cardinals agreed to play a game that the Chicago newspapers proclaimed would be for the league championship. But when the Maroons won, 21-7, the Cardinals refused to concede, instead scheduling additional games to boost the team's winning percentage. The Cardinals set their sights on a season-ending, box-office bonanza against the Chicago Bears, but figured they'd need to be in first place at the time for a shot at the season title. So the Cardinals scheduled two games before their date with the Bears, both against teams that had already folded for the year. They won both—easily, of course—topping the Milwaukee Badgers on December 10 by a score of 59-0 and the Hammond Pros two days later 13-0.

If the Cardinals continued to play and win, Pottsville realized they also would need additional victories to improve their winning percentage. So the Maroons scheduled a late December game against the Providence Steam Roller and a December 12 game against a team made up of former Notre Dame players.

The Notre Dame alumni facing the Maroons that day included the famed Four Horsemen: quarterback Harry Stuhldreher, left halfback Jim Crowley, right halfback Don Miller, and fullback Elmer Layden. They had been running roughshod over collegiate opponents since 1922, when coach Knute Rockne first put them together as sophomores. On October 18, 1924, following a 13-7 victory over Army, *New York Herald-Tribune* sportswriter Grantland Rice had granted the quartet immortality. He penned the words that are now called by the University of Notre Dame "the most famous passage in the history of sports journalism":

> Outlined against a blue, gray October sky the Four Horsemen rode again.
> In dramatic lore they are known as famine, pestilence, destruction, and
> death. These are only aliases. Their real names are: Stuhldreher, Miller,
> Crowley, and Layden. They formed the crest of the South Bend cyclone
> before which another fighting Army team was swept over the precipice
> at the Polo Grounds this afternoon as 55,000 spectators peered down
> upon the bewildering panorama spread out upon the green plain below.

Rockne's student publicity aide George Strickler, who'd later be sports editor
of the *Chicago Tribune*, made sure the new nickname stuck. He posed the players, in their uniforms, on the backs of horses. Though none of them stood over
six-feet tall, they looked larger-than-life in that now-famous photo: Stuhldreher, the cocky, feisty, and ambitious thrower who also returned punts; Crowley,
of Green Bay, Wisconsin, known as "Sleepy Jim" because he always looked
drowsy—except, that is, when he had the ball and was dodging defenders;
Miller, the breakaway threat from Defiance, Ohio, who Rockne said was the
greatest open-field runner he had ever coached; and Layden, the fastest of the
group who was known for his timely interceptions and booming punts.

The Horsemen had played thirty games together for their Catholic school
in South Bend, Indiana. They lost only twice, both times to Nebraska. They
capped off an undefeated, ten-win season in 1925 by winning the Rose Bowl;
they defeated Stanford 27-10.

Now just mere months later, under the name the All-Stars, the famed
Four Horsemen were scheduled to line up against the Pottsville Maroons, a
professional team.

When NFL President Joe Carr got wind of the game, he immediately attempted to put a stop to it. With the NFL's Frankford Yellow Jackets filing a
complaint—the game was not only to be played within Frankford's territorial
rights, it was scheduled the same day as a Frankford home game—Carr contacted Pottsville's manager.

Despite Carr's warnings, the game went ahead as scheduled. Pottsville
won. Fuming, Carr immediately fined Pottsville $500, canceled its game with
Providence, and suspended the team from the league, effectively ending any
claim the Maroons may have thought they had to the league championship.

But Carr wasn't done. He learned that Chicago-area high school players
had been used when the disbanded-for-the-year Milwaukee Badgers scram-
bled to assemble a team for their late-season tilt against the Chicago Car-

dinals. The owner of the Badgers was given ninety days to sell his team. The Cardinals were fined $1,000. And the Cardinals player who lined up the high schoolers was banned for life from the NFL.

Carr later reconsidered his punishment of the Pottsville Maroons. He decided to leave their suspension up to the league owners. Nevertheless, when the owners met on February 6, a cooled-down Carr emphatically stated his case: "Three different notices forbidding the Pottsville club to play were given and management elected to play, regardless." The owners upheld his earlier decisions. Pottsville remained booted.

The owners then turned their attention toward sorting out the flurry of late-season games and determining final standings. Even without their late-season victory over the high school players–enhanced Milwaukee Badgers, the Chicago Cardinals had the best record with eleven wins, two losses, and one tie. A motion was made to award the Cardinals the league title. But objections were raised and oppositions voiced over all the shifty, late-season wheeling and dealing. The motion was tabled. No vote was taken, and no league championship was awarded in 1925.

However, the Cardinals, with the best record, are nowadays generally accepted as the champions of the season. The Pottsville Maroons finished second with ten wins and two losses. The Green Bay Packers were ninth with eight wins and five losses. The Duluth Kelleys were sixteenth with their feeble record of zero wins and three losses. But that was still better than four other teams—including the Milwaukee Badgers, who, no matter which players they used, weren't able to muster a victory against six defeats in their second-to-last season in the NFL.

FOUR

LEAGUE VS. LEAGUE

As remarkable and thrilling as the race for the non-championship of 1925 was, it paled in comparison to the year's biggest football story. That tale had unfolded late in the season with a player who almost singlehandedly reversed the misfortunes of the struggling NFL and finally edged the upstart league toward the level and respect of the college game.

For years, the Chicago Bears' George "Papa Bear" Halas had sought a player who could attract huge gates and earn him huge profits. He believed he had finally found his man at the University of Illinois in three-time All-American Harold "Red" Grange: the "Galloping Ghost," as he was known because of his dazzling and elusive open-field running, the "miracle man of the 1920s," as the College Football Hall of Fame would dub him following his induction in 1951.

Grange, a native of Forksville, Pennsylvania, played his first game for Illinois on October 6, 1923. He dominated Nebraska with touchdown runs of fifty, thirty-five, and twelve yards. The faithful Fighting Illini fans were instantly enamored.

As a sophomore, on October 18, 1924, Grange scored four touchdowns in the first twelve minutes of a game against the University of Michigan on runs of 95, 67, 56, and 44 yards. He tallied 402 yards on the day with just twenty-one carries. The entire nation took notice.

But Grange wasn't done. He ran for 300 yards and passed for another 177 against Chicago on November 8, 1924. On Halloween 1925, he carried the ball thirty-six times for 363 yards and two touchdowns against Pennsylvania.

In all, Grange scored thirty-one touchdowns and racked up 3,362 rushing yards. Dizzying numbers, especially when one stops to consider he played just twenty collegiate games.

He was still playing them—and delivering ice during summer months—when Halas started secretly negotiating the pro contract that would send Grange and his Babe Ruth-like fame to Chicago. The deal worked out between Halas and Grange's agent and manager, the fast-talking C.C. (reportedly for "Cash and Carry") Pyle garnered the Galloping Ghost hefty shares of gate receipts. That would prove quite fair, considering the gates Grange garnered.

Just ten days after his final college game, on Thanksgiving Day 1925, Grange—an intimidating athletic specimen at six-feet tall and 180 pounds—took the field for the Bears against their crosstown rivals, the Cardinals. A standing-room-only crowd of some thirty-six thousand Chicagoans packed Wrigley Field to see the phenomenon.

The Cardinals kept an eye on him, too, limiting him to ninety-two yards rushing, fifty-six yards on punt returns and six forward passes. The crowd booed any time he didn't touch the ball. They roared when he intercepted a pass to break up his opponents' only real scoring threat of the day.

Grange reportedly earned an unheard-of $12,000 for the game, $133,683 in today's dollars.

The game ended in a scoreless draw, but the word was out. Grange and the NFL were a hot ticket. Just ten days later, more than seventy-three thousand fans crowded into New York's Polo Grounds to see Grange and the Bears play the New York Giants. The game couldn't have come at a better time for Tim Mara's Big Apple bunch. The team had been on the verge of financial collapse. The game saved the franchise.

Dreaming of more crowds like those, and sensing they had a gold mine on their hands, Halas, Pyle, and Halas' partner Dutch Sternaman arranged for the Bears to go on a barnstorming tour of the country. Starting in December, they played eight games in twelve days, five of them against NFL opponents. Stops included St. Louis, Philadelphia, New York City, Washington, Boston, Pittsburgh, and Detroit. They returned home for a final game in Chicago and then, a week later, headed out on another tour, this time to the South and the West. On January 16, 1926, more than seventy-five thousand fans filled the Los Angeles Coliseum to watch Grange and the Bears beat up on the Los Angeles Tigers.

Pro football had arrived. The nation was finally paying attention, and the NFL no longer seemed so sleazy or underhanded. Also, a blueprint for financial success had been drawn: A big name, a barnstorming tour, and a beehive of hype.

On the other side of Wisconsin from Chicago, some 470 miles away in Duluth, Minnesota, Ole Haugsrud took notice.

~

Salvation for the NFL turned sour, however, as 1925 turned to 1926. Looking to cash in while they were hot—and they'd never be hotter than in the wake of their head-turning, stadium-filling barnstorming tour—Grange and his agent approached the Bears about a new contract. They asked for a then unheard-of five-figure salary and one-third ownership of the team. Bears' owner George "Papa Bear" Halas scoffed. The demand was ridiculous, even with Grange's stardom, drawing power, and talent.

Grange and Pyle walked, taking advantage of an out clause in Grange's contract. The two had a plan.

They secured a five-year lease to play in Yankee Stadium, and then, at the NFL's February meeting in Detroit, they approached the league, requesting an expansion franchise for New York. Their pitch was compelling: the most colorful and popular player professional football had ever known playing in the nation's premiere venue. The entire league could benefit, Pyle and Grange argued.

But their request met opposition. The Giants already were playing in New York, across the Harlem River at the Polo Grounds. Giants' owner Tim Mara had a legitimate beef that a new New York team could spell doom for his year-old New York team. Plus, the league had granted Mara exclusive territorial rights in New York.

Mara won over the NFL's other owners. The league denied the request of Pyle and Grange for an expansion franchise. But the two still had a signed lease for Yankee Stadium. So they announced on the spot that they would create their own league, a rival league—the American Football League, as it would be officially called; the "Grange League," as everyone would call it.

As odd as it seemed, the Galloping Ghost, just months earlier the greatest thing ever to happen to the NFL, was now a serious threat to its very existence.

~

The AFL prepared for the 1926 season with nine teams that weren't afraid to throw around money and didn't hesitate to raid NFL rosters. They included Pyle's and Grange's New York Yankees at Yankee Stadium, which, like at least three other AFL franchises, started operations in cities already occupied by the NFL. The Chicago Bulls competed directly with the NFL's Chicago Cardinals and Chicago Bears. The AFL's Philadelphia Quakers went head-to-head with the Frankford Yellow Jackets. And the Brooklyn Horsemen—featuring Notre Dame's former Four Horsemen—joined the Yankees in giving the NFL's New York Giants competition. The Horsemen also competed with an NFL expansion franchise, the Brooklyn Lions.

Perhaps nowhere was the competition between the upstart AFL and established NFL more apparent than in Chicago. First, the Bulls leased Comiskey Park for the 1926 season, stealing the NFL Cardinal's home of many years. The Cardinals were forced to play in the smaller-venue Normal Field. The Bulls then went after the Cardinals' great halfback, John "Paddy" Driscoll, who had been lured to the Cardinals five years earlier for the outlandish annual salary of $3,000 (about $29,000 in today's figures). The Cardinals couldn't pay Driscoll the same money the Bulls now offered, but rather than losing him to the new team, the Cardinals traded him to their cross-town rivals, the Chicago Bears. The Bears grew stronger as a result and the Cardinals weaker—both on and off the field. Things got so bad financially for the Cardinals in 1926 that the team had to turn to the NFL for a break. The league obliged, rescinding the Cardinals' $1,000 fine from the previous season's game against the Milwaukee Badgers.

Other AFL teams in 1926 included the Boston Bulldogs; the Newark Bears; the Rock Island Independents, which had bolted to the new league when the NFL allowed it to suspend operations for the year; and the Cleveland Panthers, formed with the top players from the Cleveland Bulldogs, another team that had been allowed by the NFL to suspend operations for the year.

Meanwhile, the NFL plugged along in the face of the AFL challenge, also putting together their 1926 lineup. The Rochester Jeffersons and Minneapolis Marines—like the Rock Island Independents and Cleveland Bulldogs—had been granted permission to be inactive for the year, but were not snapped up by the AFL. It was the second straight year of dormancy for the Marines. But the NFL was also able to pick up six new franchises. The Hartford Blues and Los

Angeles Buccaneers were expansion clubs like the Brooklyn Lions. The league readmitted the Racine Tornadoes and welcomed back the Pottsville Maroons, mostly to keep the Maroons from also bolting to the AFL. Louisville fielded its first team in three years, but the club really had little to do with its city. The Louisville Colonels, like the new Buccaneers (and the Los Angeles Wildcats of the AFL), were a traveling team based in Chicago, at least on paper; none of them ever played in the Windy City. Buffalo changed its team's name from the Bisons to the Rangers.

The NFL had put together a healthy twenty-two teams, despite the AFL. But the threat to the NFL's existence had yet to reach its most critical moment. It wasn't when superstar Grange and Pyle announced they were creating a rival league, nor was it when the Four Horsemen of Notre Dame were signed as star players to that new league.

The darkest moment for the NFL came the day Pyle announced his AFL also had signed Ernie Nevers, the movie-star handsome All-American fullback from Stanford University—the only player who could rival Grange's immense popularity and drawing power.

~

The "Big Dog," as the wavy-haired, six foot, 205-pound Nevers was known, had been recruited out of high school by both Stanford and the University of California in Berkeley. Legend has it the recruiting war escalated until Nevers was spotted in Berkeley by zealous Stanford students; they kidnapped him and hid him away in a secluded spot along the coast—with a beautiful young woman for company—until classes had begun and he was no longer able to sign up at Cal. He had no choice but to go to Stanford, according to the legend.

Years later, Nevers told a tamer version of choosing his college, admitting Cal really was his first choice. "Brick Muller had been an idol of mine, and I got to know him," he said, referring to Cal's All-American of the early 1920s. "So I was all set to go to Cal, but at the last minute I picked Stanford. But if I had gone to Cal I probably would have stayed a lineman and nobody would have given me much of a chance. I was a terrible tackle. I did much better at fullback."

No matter how he got to Stanford, Nevers had earned eleven letters in four sports: baseball, basketball, football, and track. He was regarded as one of the greatest college pitchers of his generation, and "more than once he would go over to a track meet with his baseball uniform on and throw the javelin to win a couple of points," said Bob Murphy, the radio voice of Stanford sports. "Ernie could do everything." He even worked in Hollywood films, mostly westerns, during summer breaks from school.

But with broad shoulders, the thing he did best was play football. Running, passing, or punting, he was a phenom who excelled in all phases of the game. He was a "pile-driving runner [who was] fast enough to pull away from defenders. He supposedly was not stopped for a loss in his three years on the varsity," the San Jose, California, newspaper reported. "He never left the field." Nevers played linebacker on defense and was Stanford's kicker and punter. As a runner, he averaged five yards per carry in college. As a punter, his boots averaged forty-two yards.

Nevers was team captain in 1925 when Stanford took on its arch rival, University of California, Berkeley, a team it hadn't beaten in eight seasons. With Nevers carrying the ball on all but three of his team's offensive plays and not missing a single down on defense, Stanford put an end to the miserable streak, beating Cal 24-17.

From 1923 to 1925, Nevers led the Stanford Indians (later renamed Cardinal, no "s") to twenty-two wins against five losses and a tie. Nevers' greatest collegiate game—and the performance that cinched his stardom—was his final one: the Rose Bowl game against Notre Dame on New Year's Day 1925.

Earlier in the season, in a game against the University of Washington, Nevers had broken both of his ankles. With just days left before the Rose Bowl contest, the casts finally were removed. His coach, Glenn "Pop" Warner, fashioned braces for Nevers using scrap aluminum and pieces of inner tubing he had found in his garage at home. The braces were taped on so tightly Nevers reportedly had little feeling below his knees. Warner told him, "You'll probably last ten minutes."

But with those odd braces, and on those sore ankles, he played the entire Rose Bowl game, all sixty minutes. He even punted (somehow), matching his collegiate average of forty-two yards per boot. On defense he was involved in more than three-fourths of his team's tackles. On offense he passed for 138 yards, 8 yards more than the entire Notre Dame team. And he ran the ball a Rose Bowl record thirty-four times for 114 yards, only 13 yards less than the combined total of Notre Dame's famed backfield, the Four Horsemen.

Time and again, Nevers led his team down the field. At one point, with Stanford threatening to score, the Fighting Irish defenders were relieved to see a player being sent in from the sideline. Surely, he'd have instructions from Rockne about how to stop Nevers. But all the player could stammer was: "Boys, Rock says the trouble is you're not stopping Nevers."

But Nevers wasn't perfect. With a capacity crowd of fifty-three thousand fans hooting and hollering, he tossed two interceptions, both returned for touchdowns by Notre Dame's Layden. Despite Nevers' heroics, the Stanford Indians came up short, 27-10.

Even with the loss, Warner, who had coached Jim Thorpe at Carlisle, said Nevers was the best back he ever coached, the greatest all-around man football had ever known, and a "player without a fault.... Nevers could do everything Thorpe could and he always tried harder. Ernie gave sixty minutes of himself every game."

"What would that man have done if he'd been healthy?" Notre Dame Coach Knute Rockne marveled after the game. "Nevers could do everything. He tore our line to shreds, ran the ends, forward passed, and kicked." He called Nevers "the greatest fullback of all time."

"That game has stuck in my memory," Nevers told the Associated Press' Claude Burgett in a 1965 interview about that Rose Bowl game. "Stanford lost, but I gained some lifetime friends."

∼

Before graduating from Stanford, Nevers had left school to play professionally in a special series of exhibition games with Red Grange.

"He was practically denounced from the pulpit," the San Francisco Examiner's Rick Setlowe wrote in the summer of 1964. "In those days, pro football was considered only slightly more legitimate than, say, bootlegging, and hardly the profession for an All-American from Stanford."

"But I needed the money," Nevers countered in the cover story. "All we got at college in those days was a hashing job. I got a little help on the tuition, [even though] it was only $90 a quarter then, [but] I was still in debt. And so was my father. Those exhibition games took the mortgage off my family's ranch."

Following graduation, Nevers' jersey number—"1"—was the first at Stanford ever to be retired. He then signed contracts to play professional basketball and to pitch for professional baseball's St. Louis Browns. He also signed on to play for Pyle's American Football League, teaming up again with Red Grange, at a reported annual salary of $15,000 (about $167,000 in today's figures).

At least that's what Pyle told everyone. In Duluth, Minnesota, Ole Haugsrud wasn't buying it.

~

Haugsrud assumed co-ownership of the franchise in 1926. "After our experiences of 1925, the players were really disgusted," Haugsrud told *Duluth News Tribune* sportswriter Bruce Bennett fifty years later. "They wanted to get out of the ownership of the club. They didn't want to have to continue to dip into their own pockets after a game to pay the bills."

A financially stable Haugsrud took over the team with manager Dewey Scanlon. "I had the honor of being the manager, secretary-treasurer, paymaster, and in fact general factotum for this squad," Haugsrud wrote.

He and Scanlon made the transaction legal by handing the player-owners one crisp dollar bill. The players immediately raced to a Duluth tavern, the story goes, and spent their buck on twenty nickel beers. "It would be a drunken hangover they would all one day regret," Ross Bernstein wrote in *Pigskin Pride*.

Along with the assetts of a professional football team, Haugsrud and Scanlon "assumed the club's bills, too, and to partially defray them we sold Mickey McDonnell, a great little halfback who had starred previously at Duluth Cathedral High, to the Chicago Cardinals for $300, and Bill Rooney, a mighty backfield man to the New York Giants for $100," Haugsrud wrote in a 1963 team history.

The NFL had no draft in the 1920s, and the best players tended to wind up with the league's top franchises, such as Green Bay, Chicago, and Philadelphia. Many teams preferred to schedule games with other teams whose rosters included former college stars. Knowing this, Haugsrud got to thinking. He thought of Grange and his barnstorming success in Chicago. He thought about the contract the AFL supposedly had with Nevers. And he came up with a strategy.

He called together his players in Duluth. "We had a meeting," he said. "I spelled out my plan. I was going to try to sign Nevers. The team was willing to try anything."

Haugsrud had reason to be optimistic about wooing Nevers, a rising star with the world at his doorstep, to Duluth, the NFL's most-remote venue: It just so happened that Ole Haugsrud and Ernie Nevers had grown up together right next door to Duluth in Superior.

~

Ernest Alonzo Nevers had been born on June 11, 1903, in Willow River, Minnesota, about fifty miles south of Superior. His parents managed the old Northern Hotel. While he was still a boy—and big for his age, according to family and friends—the Nevers family moved to Moose Lake, Minnesota, where he played amateur baseball, and then to Superior. His parents ran a boarding house in Superior's Allouez neighborhood.

In 1917, a fourteen-year-old Nevers decided to try out for the Superior Central High School football team, never mind that he "didn't know a football from a squash," as he admitted later. Other players immediately picked up how green he was. "Go back to the farm," some of them jeered, urging Nevers to turn in his jersey.

But Nevers, joined by his good friend Ole Haugsrud, persisted. His first role in practice, he said, was tackling dummy. "I used to stand in the sawdust pits and let the other kids tackle and block me," he said. Haugsrud recalled those training sessions in a 1973 interview:

> I stood on one sawdust pit and Ernie on the other.... We just stood there, and one by one every other guy on the team took his turn at banging into us. Eventually, though, Ernie's size and ability as a football player showed through and he was put on the first team. Me? I think I wound up on the sixth [team].

Superior Central Coach Ira Tubbs played Nevers at tackle. He was a "demon" on defense, according to reports. Along with his older teammates, Nevers, a sophomore, and the Superior Central Vikings won the 1918 Wisconsin State Football Championship. They outscored their opponents 427-7. In one drubbing, they beat Duluth Denfeld High Shcool 117-0. A year later, they won the sectional championship.

Nevers also excelled on the hard court. In fact, basketball was probably his better sport in those days. Some have credited him with inventing the hook shot while still in high school. Nevers' 1920 Superior Central team lost only once during the regular season, to Duluth Central, en route to another Wisconsin state championship. Nevers and his teammates John "Bone" Hancock and Basil Christmas were named to the all-state team.

Just prior to Nevers' senior year, his family moved to a ranch in Santa Rosa, California. His new high school there was just launching football for the first time. He quickly realized he knew more than the coach and designed the offense, putting himself at fullback. "You see, I wanted every chance to carry the ball and kick," he said. The team won a conference championship, and college scouts started taking notice of Nevers.

During the opening days of the basketball season, Nevers unexpectedly left California and returned, on his own, to Superior. He helped his old Superior Central Vikings to third place in the state basketball tourney and dreamed of collegiate glory playing for the University of Wisconsin in Madison.

But when his father insisted he return to his family in California, Nevers headed west once again, enrolling at Santa Rosa Junior College where he helped to organize the school's first football team. From there, he transferred to Stanford where, in addition to being known as "Big Dog," he was sometimes called the "Blond Bull" because of his sun-washed hair and muscular thighs. As quiet as his Midwestern roots off the field, Nevers was ferocious and intense when in competition.

~

In the summer of 1926, Haugsrud found his former classmate in St. Louis pitching for the Browns after a minor-league stint earlier in the year with the San Francisco Missions.

"Ernie was very glad to see me and I was glad to see him," Haugsrud told Myron Cope, author of *The Game That Was*.

Inside the apartment he shared with his wife, Nevers produced a letter he had received from C. C. Pyle of the American Football League. It was accompanied by a contract, promising to pay Nevers $15,000 for the season. Haugsrud noted immediately that his hunch was correct: The contract wasn't signed.

"Ole, if you can meet the terms Pyle is offering in this letter, it's OK with me. I'll play for Duluth," Nevers said.

Haugsrud agreed, sweetening Nevers' $15,000 salary by offering him 10 percent of the team's larger gate receipts.

"I had the money to do it," Haugsrud told Cope. "I believe I was only twenty-two or twenty-three years old, but I had various holdings—buildings and things like that. I had inherited a little money."

He hadn't brought much cash with him to St. Louis, however. Nevers inked his name to a contract sans a signing bonus. "Oh, maybe I gave him a dollar to make it legal, but really a handshake was all Ernie wanted," Haugsrud recalled. "A handshake with an old friend was good enough for Ernie."

Returning to Duluth, a jubilant Haugsrud asked the Kelleys who were in the Twin Ports, about ten of them, to gather in the Superior dental office of Doc Kelly.

Haugsrud told them he had done what some of them probably believed was impossible: He had signed Nevers to play for Duluth. He shared with the team the salary he agreed to pay Nevers.

"Here's what it is," he said of the contract. "Now how much do you guys want?"

"I left it up to them," Haugsrud recalled. "They were probably the only team that ever drew up their own contracts. But it was very, very easy for me to do this because they wanted to play."

"We'd have played for board and room and dry socks if we had to," Bill Stein told the *Duluth News Tribune* in 1963. He and Art Johnson said they were paid $75 to $85 per game on average during their days in Duluth.

Haugsrud told his players he'd step out of the room so they could "make up their minds."

"But I no more got out the door when they called me back," he recalled. "Actually, I think they'd had it all worked out."

Doc Williams rose to his feet, towering above his gathered teammates, to speak on behalf of everyone. "Well, how does this sound? Fifty dollars [if we] lose, sixty dollars [when we] tie, and seventy-five [for a] win?"

"That's OK," Haugsrud quickly answered. "Now if you don't mind, I'll take this as an option and go down to the league meeting in Chicago and see what I can do about a schedule."

FIVE

DULUTH SAVES THE NFL

The NFL's league meeting in August 1926 was held in Chicago's Morrison Hotel. The opulent landmark, a New Year's Eve favorite among upper-crust, champagne-sipping Chicagoans, had just completed its latest expansion. Its signature, forty-six-story tower was under construction and a year from completion. When done, the Morrison would boast itself as the "World's Tallest Hotel."

With its tower and flagpole reaching 637 feet into the air, it certainly was one of the tallest buildings on the Chicago skyline. And one of the city's most elegant. Many of its 2,500 rooms—each with private baths, a true test of "upscale" in the early 1900s—offered unbeatable views of Lake Michigan. Its choice of restaurants included a dinner theater, and its lobbies featured marble floors, a marble front desk, rich wood-paneled walls, and cast-bronze ornamentation.

With a secret in his bag, Haugsrud's strut had to be triumphant as he made his way through the Morrison's lush lobby. The first person he sought out after arriving in Chicago was New York Giants owner Tim Mara, who was "like a father to me from the beginning," as Haugsrud said in *The Game That Was*. He told Mara how he'd been able to sign Nevers away from the rival American Football League. Mara urged him not to tell the other owners.

Not yet.

"I'll tell you kid," Mara said, "we've got to do something here to make this a league. Now we'll go through with the regular meeting, and when it gets halfway through and you [have] two, three ballgames [scheduled] I will give you the high sign."

The meeting got under way, and "here everybody was, sitting with the threat that Pyle had hanging over them," as Haugsrud recalled. "The league really didn't know if it was going to operate again."

On Mara's signal, which came as planned just as discussions started about the upcoming season's schedule, Haugsrud approached league president Joe Carr. He delivered his news, including that his team had a new name: "Ernie Nevers' Eskimos."

Carr stopped the meeting. "Gentlemen, I've got a surprise for you," he said. He relayed the news to the room.

"Everyone figured that Pyle not only had Grange and Wildcat Wilson and the Four Horsemen of Notre Dame, but Ernie Nevers, too. So all those people at the meeting cheered, and there was almost a celebration right there," Haugsrud said. "Some of them out front got up and yelled like a bunch of kids."

In the delirium, Carr rushed back to Haugsrud and vigorously shook his hand. "Young man," he said, "you've just saved the National Football League."

Mara quieted his fellow owners and made a proposal to begin paying Carr a salary "that means something." The league president's compensation was increased on the spot from $500 to $2,500.

The owners then ripped up the schedules of games they had just begun to put together and started from scratch. Nevers had changed everything.

"The way they would do it was you would name a date, and Mara would ask another club owner, 'Would you like to play him on that date?' And the club owner would say 'yes' or 'no,' and you got whatever games you could," Haugsrud explained. "Well, we started putting down that 1926 schedule and I had nineteen league games as fast as I could write them down. And before I got back to Duluth, I had ten exhibition games which made a total of twenty-nine [games]. And all because I had Nevers. Some of [the other teams] wanted two games with us." Signing Nevers "gave us our attraction, our meal ticket," Haugsrud said in a 1974 newspaper interview. "We no longer had any trouble scheduling games." (Haugsrud may have misremembered slightly; the Eskimos would actually play 14 league games and 15 exhibitions during that season.)

But while the other NFL franchises were eager for a date with Nevers and the Eskimos, they weren't necessarily thrilled by the prospect of traveling to and playing in often-chilly and often-foggy, far-northern Duluth. Not only was Athletic Park uncomfortable, but Duluth in the mid-1920s wasn't yet the visitors' paradise it would become. Canal Park, the heart of Duluth's now-bustling tourism industry, wasn't filled yet with trendy restaurants, wood-floored souvenir shops, and public art, but with scrap-iron yards, hardware manufacturers, grocery wholesalers, whorehouses, and rough-and-tumble taverns.

The league decided to designate the Eskimos a "road team."

"We've got to…fill the ballparks in the big cities," Mara said. The owners agreed, knowing Nevers could help do that. They didn't even flinch when Haugsrud demanded a guarantee for him and his team of $4,000 per game plus a percentage of the gate receipts over $8,000.

Imagine Haugsrud's strut when he made his way back through the marble-rich lobby of the Morrison Hotel and disappeared into the Chicago skyline. He could wear a grin of satisfaction all the way back home to the Twin Ports.

~

Knowing his team was about to hit the road for months on end, Haugsrud, the master marketer, decided the players needed new uniforms—memorable duds that would leave little doubt about who the grid stars were or where they were from. At a time when most teams' jerseys featured the players' numbers on the front and little else, Haugsrud's standout shirt design included using midnight blue to mark the shoulders, cuffs, and forearm bands of an otherwise white jersey. Its most striking feature was a distinctive white igloo across the chest set against a seven-sided polygon, also in midnight blue. The pants were grey.

He provided the players with custom-imprinted traveling trunks for all their gear, each with "ERNIE NEVERS' ESKIMOS" and "DULUTH, MINN." stenciled to the sides.

And to complete his Eskimos' image-is-everything makeover, Haugsrud arranged to outfit his players with custom-tailored, oversized, double-breasted, thigh-length mackinaw coats to wear when they were on the sidelines and while traveling. The large white overcoats became a team trademark, each with an igloo shape and the words "ERNIE NEVERS' ESKIMOS" and "DULUTH" splashed across the back. The coats were produced for the team by Frederick A. Patrick, "a liberal-minded clothing manufacturer," as Haugsrud once described him, and "one of the greatest boosters Duluth ever had."

Patrick also did just about as much as the Eskimos in putting Duluth on the national map in the 1920s. He made the city famous as a manufacturer of mackinaws in the 1910s and 1920s when the super-light and toasty-warm garments, once worn only by lumberjacks, were embraced by college students, businessmen, and others. Patrick's lasting legacy, and his most famous garment, was the midnight blue-and-white mackinaw he produced for the Eskimos in 1926. "Those coats sure made a hit with the fans from coast to coast," Haugsrud wrote in 1963. One of the originals hangs to this day in the Pro Football Hall of Fame in Canton, Ohio.

~

Before launching into their team's lengthy 1926 game schedule, Haugsrud and Scanlon scored another NFL first: a preseason training camp.

They considered Moose Lake, Minnesota, and Solon Springs, Wisconsin, for what they expected would be three weeks of intensive practices. But after "considerable dickering" with the leaders of those small communities and others around the Head of the Lakes region, they settled on training in Two Harbors, the *Duluth News Tribune*'s Cubby Campbell reported. The sleepy Minnesota port town and railroad hub, onced defined by its ore docks, sits about twenty miles northeast of Duluth along the rocky Lake Superior shoreline.

As many as twenty players—or prospective players—were expected to report to the grand brownstone Spalding Hotel in downtown Duluth at 8 A.M., Monday, September 5, 1926, and then travel together to the camp aboard a bus bouncing along what was then Highway 1 or the North Shore Scenice Drive (it would become the northern-most stretch of Highway 61 in 1934).

Camp headquarters were established at Hotel Agate in Two Harbors and in the American Legion hall in the hotel's basement. The hotel, at First Street and Waterfront Drive, later became an apartment building known as Agate Manor. Some players may have stayed at the Rustic Inn, according to *Two Harbors 100 Years: A Pictorial History of Two Harbors and Surrounding Communities*. A renowned hamburger stand after it was built in 1923, the Rustic Inn and its cabins later housed Civilian Conservation Corps camp workers and catered to hay fever sufferers when they flocked for relief from farm country to the cool breezes along Lake Superior's North Shore in the days before antihistamines.

Each day of camp started with a three-mile run or hike and then a hearty early morning breakfast. The meal proved heartier for some players than others. Lineman Oke Carlson reportedly downed twenty-four eggs one morning—and then chased them with a slab of steak.

Morning drills started at 8:30 A.M. at the athletic field in Two Harbors named for Horace Johnson, president of the Duluth and Iron Range Railway from 1926 to 1930. Morning practices ended around 11 A.M., followed by lunch, and then afternoon practices ran from 1:30 P.M. to 5 P.M. After dinner, the players gathered in makeshift classrooms to diagram, study, and learn plays. Practices were held twice a day "to get the players on edge," team manager Scanlon told Campbell.

Although the training was regimented and typical of the regimens followed by many elite college teams of the day—complete with training tables, strict "bed checks," and a close adherence to "lights out"—"camp was a raucous, yet physically demanding time," according to author Ross Bernstein.

The first day's practices, on September 7, 1926, were held in a steady drizzle. The weather restricted drills to the basics: kicking, punting, and charging. Nevertheless, Scanlon saw enough to declare his entire squad in fine physical shape, the players' legs strong, their stamina healthy following several weeks of light training on their own.

"There will be an abundance of beef in the Eskimo squad this season if the members who started work Tuesday prove an example of what the entire squad will be like," Campbell wrote after taking his first glimpse of the Duluth gridders. "With one exception, every man on the squad is tall and rangy. The lone exception is Paul Fitzgibbon, the brilliant halfback from Creighton University, who is short and compactly built, tipping the scales at 170 [pounds]."

Although physically different from his teammates, Fitzgibbon, a native of Sioux Falls, South Dakota, wasn't an exception when it came to ability. A wire that arrived on the first day of camp provided proof of that. Chicago Bears' owner George "Papa Bear" Halas, inquired whether Duluth would be willing to trade or outright sell the "Red-Haired Flash," as Fitzgibbon was called. Scanlon took one look at the paper and "shot back an answer," Cubby Campbell reported. "Nothing doing."

Nevers was a no-show on the first day; he had left the St. Louis Browns' baseball club and traveled north by car, expecting to arrive in Duluth a day before camp started. He assumed he'd make such good time that he'd be able to visit family in Moose Lake before reporting to Duluth. Stormy weather held him up, however, and after visiting his sister in Moose Lake he arrived the day after camp kicked off.

In all, fifteen players participated on that first day of drills. The ranks included one unidentified player, a "mystery player," as Campbell called the athlete he didn't recognize. Scanlon declined to divulge any information.

Until the next day, that is, when the player finally signed a contract. Johnny Blood was the name, Scanlon said. The Eskimos obtained him from Minneapolis. He was "one of the greatest pro backs and one of the most colorful," Haugsrud said. "He was truly brilliant, both physically and mentally, but a trifle unpredictable."

How appropriate that Blood's introduction to Duluth and the Eskimos would be shrouded in a bit of mystery.

~

Johnny Blood wasn't even the real name of the halfback who started practice with the Eskimos before even signing a contract to play. He had stolen the name from a movie theater marquee to protect a year of college eligibility.

The real name of the hard-playing, hard-drinking, future hall of famer was John Victor McNally. He "would have made Brett Favre seem like an introverted librarian," as Doug Moe of the Madison, Wisconsin, *Capital Times* once wrote. He was "Paul Hornung, if Hornung had read Herman Melville [or] Brett Favre, if Favre could debate Thomas Malthus' theory of economics."

McNally was born the fourth of six surviving children on November 27, 1903, in New Richmond, Wisconsin, about thirty-five miles from St. Paul. His mother, a sophisticated and educated woman who broke colts in her spare time, pushed him to study. His father, a boxing and baseball fan who managed the New Richmond Roller Mills, pushed him to entertain.

McNally spent his childhood running and climbing—trees, telephone poles, anything. At age four, he climbed out his bedroom window and to the peak of his family's three-story Queen Anne–styled home. His father fetched a ladder to get him down. At age twelve, he leaped, on a dare, from the top of a railroad bridge and into a river. To amuse himself, he and his friends hopped aboard trains that daily rolled through their town, jumping off after a few blocks.

"I suppose I must have a strong need for attention," McNally once told sports historian Ralph Hickok. "I can't explain some of the things I've done on any other basis."

A bright student, McNally "blazed through New Richmond rather than growing up there," Denis J. Gullickson wrote in an excellent 2006 biography,

Vagabond Halfback. He graduated high school at age fourteen and went off to River Falls Normal School, about twenty miles to the south. There, he lost interest in books—temporarily, he said—and discovered girls. "I was away from home and feeling my oats," he told Hickok. For the first time in his life his grades slipped.

His studies became such a lost cause he climbed onto a freight train one day and headed for South Dakota where his uncle owned a farm. The following fall, he eagerly abandoned farm work and enrolled at St. John's University in Collegeville, a remote town in the middle of Minnesota. He developed an interest in running, and he wrote essays for the college newspaper, *The Record*.

In the fall of 1920, McNally played organized football for the first time. The captain of an intramural team spotted him running on the campus track and noted how fast he was.

"By himself more than by extensive coaching, McNally learned how to plan elementary plays; to drop kick; to run in a twisting, crazy-legged fashion; to struggle when tackled and to always fall forward after dragging the tackler as far as he could," wrote Tom Roeser, a former St. John's student and a reporter for the *Minnesota Daily Times* in St. Cloud.

In addition to playing football, McNally was a starting center and the captain of the St. John's basketball team. He was the first St. John's athlete to earn letters in four sports: football, basketball, baseball, and track.

In spring 1921, McNally cleared a high jump of five feet six and one-half inches and took first place in a state meet. At the annual Memorial Field Day Celebration, he earned the most individual points and was presented the silver loving cup. He handed it to his father, who was suffering from melancholia brought on by ennui and advancing age. Winning the cup and giving it to his father would be the most satisfying moment in athletics for McNally.

That summer, his father died. "My first thought is that it was such a terrible tragedy, such a waste," McNally recalled during a conversation with Hickok. "I had a great admiration for him. I thought he was a great guy, and we were good friends. My second thought was, 'Now he can see me. He can watch everything I do, and he can see what a son-of-a-bitch I am.'"

McNally's greatest feat at St. John's came on a baseball diamond. "John set his sights on pitching a game, though he'd never done this in the past," Gullickson wrote. "John went to Sunday Mass...with a baseball and Christy Matthewson's book on pitching.... There in church that day, under the watchful eye of the Great Umpire, he began practicing the proper finger positions for the various pitches." Three days later, McNally took the mound against Macalester, giving up three hits and leading St. John's to victory over its rivals from St. Paul.

A headline in a Minneapolis newspaper asked, "Is there anything Mac can't do?"

McNally thought he'd find out. He enrolled in the autumn of 1923 at the University of Notre Dame in South Bend, Indiana. He joined legendary Coach Knute Rockne and the Four Horsemen on the gridiron. But the coaches switched him from tailback to tackle and he became "a guy lost in the line," Gullickson wrote.

"A tackle's job is to seek contact," McNally complained to assistant coach George Keogan. "A halfback's job is to avoid contact. I think my talent, if I have any, lies in avoiding contact." McNally's lone contribution to the annals of Fighting Irish football would be his writing of English poetry papers for Harry Stuhldreher, one of the Four Horsemen. He spent that fall playing football for the South Bend YMCA, and he took an apartment off campus, a violation of school rules.

A final run-in ended his days at America's premiere Catholic university. On St. Patrick's Day 1924 McNally joined a street celebration. The crowd swelled and a streetcar was turned onto its side. The crowd dispersed, fleeing in all directions. But not McNally. The authorities grabbed him and Notre Dame suspended him. Across his transcripts, someone wrote, "Gone—Never to Return!"

McNally made sure of it. He plunked down $125 for a used four-cylinder Ace motorcycle that he pointed east where his sisters Lucille and Honor were setting sail to Europe. He figured he'd see them off. On the back of his bike for the road trip was a "hot married blonde he'd met at a dance and taken to his apartment," as Gullickson reported. McNally, in a recorded interview, said he met the eighteen-year-old woman at a party in South Bend: "I told her I had purchased a motorcycle and was planning a tour of the Eastern seaboard. She confided that she was married to a sailor who was due to sail from Norfolk, and she was anxious to wish him bon voyage. So we set out."

The two spent nights sleeping on park benches. They pawned her jewelry for gas money, and he did odd jobs to buy sandwiches. When no money could be found, the hot blonde ditched the adventure and McNally ditched the bike.

He hopped trains to Washington, D.C., where he ran up and down the steps of the Washington Monument before heading to New York to visit old friends from Notre Dame and his sister Helen, who was in summer school at Radcliffe College.

"Maybe I was the first hippie, just forty years ahead of my time," McNally told Hickok. "I was drifting along in the sense that I was looking for my lifestyle, as they say nowadays."

His lifestyle was football, as he was about to find out.

Back home in Minnesota, McNally went to work for the *Tribune*, his uncle's Minneapolis newspaper. If he was willing to work his way up, his uncle had told him, someday he could be owner. McNally started out hauling stereotypes, the heavy printing plates that were set on the presses and later had to be removed to be melted down. He worked with an old friend from St. John's, Ralph Hanson, and one day the two of them spotted an ad in their paper for able-bodied men to try out for a semi-pro football team called the East 26th Street Liberties. With the promise of $6 per game, McNally and Hanson hopped on McNally's motorcycle after work and headed for the practice field.

Both were eligible to play one more year of college football, something that would be taken away if they were caught accepting money to play professionally. McNally hadn't even totally ruled out a return to Notre Dame. They needed aliases, and as they motored south on Minneapolis' Hennepin Avenue and turned onto Seventh Street on their way to the practice field off Nicollet Avenue, they found them. The marquee of the Garrick Theater advertised Rudolph Valentino's newest movie: "Blood and Sand."

"That's it," McNally declared. "I'll be 'Blood' and you be 'Sand.'"

Hickok asked McNally if he realized just how striking a name he had latched onto with "Johnny Blood."

"No, not consciously," McNally responded. "But I can't speak for my subconscious. The idea was probably lurking around in there somewhere. You never really know what your subconscious is doing, and it's always up to something."

With McNally playing tailback well enough to be named at the end of the year to the citywide all-star team, the Liberties won the city championship—and attracted the attention of bigger teams. But first McNally took a one-fight detour into boxing. "I only wanted to find out whether I can fight,"

McNally said. He showed promise in three rounds with Johnny Anderson, a middleweight champion who hadn't lost in fifty bouts.

McNally was contacted in the late summer of 1925 by the Ironwood Miners of Michigan's Upper Peninsula. They offered him $60 per game to run the football. McNally accepted, leaving behind a bewildered family and the promise of an ownership in the *Tribune*. "I wanted to be able to do something I enjoyed and something that would leave me enough leisure time to do other things that I enjoyed," McNally explained to Hickok. "The family, I'm sure, thought I was being lazy [and] afraid of work. But that wasn't it. I've worked hard at a lot of jobs. I worked hard at being a stereographer. What I wanted was freedom, and freedom meant to me being allowed to choose what I wanted to do."

He played three games for Ironwood, including one contest against the Kelley-Duluth team. "The games were rough as hell but the parties after the games were even rougher," McNally told Hickok. "Both teams would usually go over to Hurley [in neighboring Wisconsin] to drink, and the brawls that started during the game would resume right where they'd been left off."

The NFL's Milwaukee Badgers were the next professional team to take note of McNally's blinding speed and open-field elusiveness. They offered him $75 a game, and he jumped at it.

In a game against the Akron Pros, McNally lined up across from Olympic sprinter and broad jumper Sol Butler. In an early play—and a sign of things to come—McNally outran Butler, hauled in a pretty pass, and raced fifty-five yards for a touchdown.

But the Badgers fell into disarray late in the 1925 season. After disbanding for the season, the team agreed to one last game against the Chicago Cardinals and illegally used high school players to fill out its roster. Milwaukee's team owner was ordered to sell his franchise. Not wanting anything to do with the mess, Blood McNally bolted for California where he worked on Catalina Island as a bouncer and as a "stick man" who handled the dice on crap tables.

He thought maybe he was out of football for good. But then Haugsrud and the Ernie Nevers' Eskimos came calling. The Eskimos, Gullickson wrote, were "probably the most colorful [team] to ever do battle in the NFL. They were often called a team of vagabonds."

What better place for a vagabond halfback?

This muddy photo, scanned from a yellowed and faded newspaper, once belonged to Eskimos' owner Ole Haugsrud. It shows the 1924 Kelley-Duluth Hardware football team, which became the Duluth Eskimos in 1926. Top row, from left: Sam Kearnes (trainer), Wally Gilbert, Dewey Scanlon (manager), and M.C. Gebert (president); middle, from left: Art Johnson, Joe Sternaman (coach and quarterback), Allen McDonald, Russell Method, Bunk Harris, Bill Rooney, and Roddy Dunn; bottom from left: Joe Rooney, Howard Kiley, Max Morris, "Doc" Williams, Joe Madigan, Bill Stein, Ted (Ira) Haaven, Dick O'Donnell; at bottom center is Bill Bloedel, the team mascot.
Photo courtesy Dick Palmer and the Duluth Budgeteer.

A vintage postcard captures an aerial view of Duluth's ore docks, where the city's West End (a.k.a. "Lincoln Park") meets West Duluth, sometime between 1900 and 1915. The field in the foreground was the local racing track, built on land provided by Wheeler Lumber on the site where the Wheeler Field softball facility stands today. Between the race track and the bay you can see Athletic Park, where the Kelley-Duluth team played its home games (and where the Eskimos played their single home game). In 1941 Wade Stadium was built at the Athletic Park site for the Duluth Dukes, the local minor league baseball team. Today "The Wade" is home to the Duluth Huskies minor league baseball team. **Image from the X-communication archive.**

In 1896 Michael Hugh Kelley (above), founded Kelley-Duluth Hardware, offering "miners' and mill supplies, hardware and other merchandise commonly sold in hardware stores." Little did he suspect that in 1923 sporting goods manager Marshall C. Gebert would form the Kelley-Duluth football team, the predecessor to the Duluth Eskimos.
Photo courtesy the Duluth Public Library.

Bobby "Rube" Marshall, a University of Minnesota standout, one of the first two black men to play in the NFL, and a member of the 1925 Kelley-Duluth team. Marshall was 45 years old when he suited up for Duluth (to protect his ribs, he stuffed washboards under his uniform). In 1971, Marshall was posthumously inducted into the College Football Hall of Fame.
Photo from the College Football Hall of Fame.

Kelley-Duluth Hardware (sign at bottom left) at its 1925 location in the Bradley Building at the southeast corner of Superior Street and Lake Avenue; the hardware store ended its sponsorship in 1926, the Eskimos' first year. **Photo courtesy the Duluth Public Library.**

These vintage postcards show the McKay Hotel (above) and its lodge-like lobby (below). After games and practices, the Duluth players often washed up at the McKay, which was at 430 West First Street (where the *Duluth News Tribune* building now stands). The hotel—a brick building adorned with awnings over the sidewalks and illuminated by gas-powered lamps—served as clubhouse, training quarters and dressing room, according to players. In the same building was a drug store and "Turkish Baths." Across First Street from the hotel, on a square block now occupied by the Duluth Civic Center with its fountains, City Hall, the St. Louis County courthouse, and the Gerald W. Heaney Federal Building, was a gas-lit field where the Duluth team held practices. **Image from the X-communication archive.**

The 1926 Duluth Eskimos (a.k.a. "Ernie Nevers' Eskimos") posing in their custom-made mackinaw jackets at training camp in Two Harbors, Minnesota (even though the photo identifies the location as "Duluth"; both locations are in doubt as neither town was known to have a facility like the one the team is standing before). From left: Ole Haugsrud (owner), Walt "Chet" Gayer, Dewey Scanlon, Walt Kiesling, Russ Method, "Jock" Murray, "Porky" Rundquist, Joe Rooney, Ernie Nevers, Art Johnson, Jack Underwood, "Cobb" Rooney, Bill Stein, Johnny "Blood" McNally, James Manion, "Oke" Carlson, and Paul Fitzgibbon (not shown: Charles "Doc" Kelly, "Red" Sullivan, "Doc" Williams, "Red" Quam, Jimmy Manion, and Wally Gilbert).
Photo courtesy the Two Harbors Public Library via the Lake County Historical Society.

The Hotel Agate in Two Harbors, Minnesota, where the 1926 Duluth Eskimos reportedly stayed during the 1926 training camp—the first-ever training camp held by an NFL team. Other reports suggest the team may have stayed at the Rustic Inn, also in Two Harbors. The hotel is now the Agate Manor apartment complex.
Photo courtesy the Two Harbors Public Library via the Lake County Historical Society.

These images from the Eskimos' 1926 training camp in Two Harbors, Minnesota—not seen since 1926—were found on microfilm editions of the *Duluth News Tribune*, which explains their poor condition. **Top left:** Walter "Chet" Gayer leaps over a would-be tackler; **top right:** Ernie Nevers takes a knee; **bottom:** "Doc" Williams poses as a snapper. **Images from the X-communication archive.**

This array of Eskimos mugshots appeared in the *Duluth News Tribune* the day of their first game in 1926, an exhibition in Superior, Wisconsin, in which they defeated the Gogebic Panthers of Ironwood & Bessemer, Michigan. The Eskimos: #1 Ernie Nevers, #2 Jack Underwood, #3 Bill Stein, #4 "Doc" Kelly, #5 Cobb Rooney, #6 "Red" Sullivan, #7 Walt Gayer, #8 "Oke" Carlson, #9 Russ Method, #10 Walt Kiesling, #11 "Red" Quam, #12 "Porky" Rundquist, #13 Paul Fitzgibbon, #14 Joe Rooney, and #15 Art Johnson. Not shown: "Doc" Williams, Johnny "Blood" McNally, and Jimmy Manion, who joined the team just several days before the game. Also of note, "Doc" Kelly and other players who attended training camp—"Red" Sullivan, and "Red" Quam—were not featured on the postcard on the facing page. **Image from the X-communication archive.**

Ernie Nevers

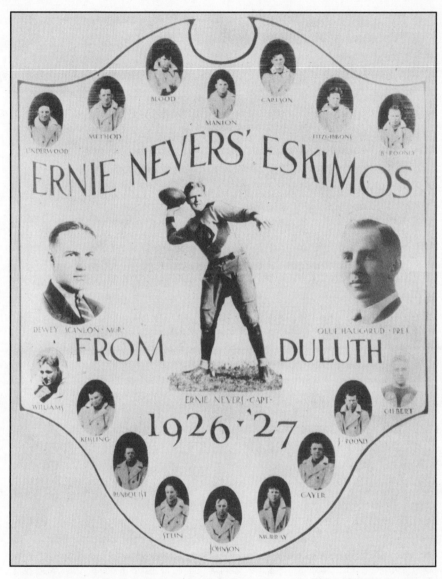

A "postcard" made to promote the 1926 Duluth Eskimos—often billed as "Ernie Nevers' Eskimos" to cash in on their star's national recognition. Captain Nevers poses at center, flanked by manager Dewey Scanlon and owner Ole Haugsrud, who persuaded Nevers to join the Duluth team, a move credited as saving the NFL. Top from left: Jack Underwood, Russ Method, Johnny "Blood" McNally, Jimmy Manion, "Oke" Carlson, Paul Fitzgibbon, and Bill Rooney; bottom from left: "Doc" Williams, Walt Kiesling, "Porky" Rundquist, Bill Stein, Art Johnson, "Jock" Murray, Walt "Chet" Gayer, Joe Rooney, and Wally Gilbert. While James Manion is shown in the training camp photo on page 70, he and other players who attended training camp—"Doc" Kelly, "Red" Sullivan, and "Red" Quam—were not featured on this piece. **Photo courtesy the Duluth Public Library.**

The images above are from the first game the Duluth Eskimos ever played, an exhibition against the Gogebic Panthers of Ironwood and Bessemer, Michigan, played at Hislop Field in Superior, Wisconsin. The Eskimos beat the Panthers by a score of 25–0. Not seen since 1926, the photographs were found on microfilm editions of the *Duluth News Tribune*, which explains their poor condition.

Top: "Doc" Kelly, a dentist from Superior, starting a play that brought Duluth its first touchdown; Ernie Nevers can be seen clearing the way for the halfback.

Middle: Kelly scoring the first touchdown of the game; referee Art Voz bends over the play to make the call.

Bottom: In the first quarter Nevers, unable to find an open receiver, eludes three tacklers and skirts down the right flank for a twenty-five-yard gain.

Image from the X-communication archive.

More images from the first game the Duluth Eskimos ever played. **Top:** Paul Fitzgibbon gains fifteen yards for the Eskimos in the first quarter. **Middle:** Nevers at the start of a plunge play; he crashed through off right tackle to gain eight yards. **Bottom:** Nevers being tackled by two Panther defenders; as always Nevers fought forward even while being taken down.

Image from the X-communication archive.

Two photographs of Ernie Nevers, the star of the Duluth Eskimos and, in college, a three-sport All-American at Stanford. **Photos courtesy Lake Superior Magazine via Barry Singer.**

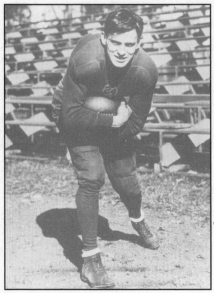

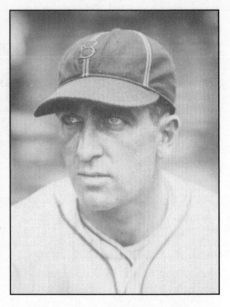

Johnny "Blood" McNally—the notorious "Vagabond Halfback"—in his Green Bay Packers uniform (above) and in a photo collage on display at the Green Bay Packers Hall of Fame at Green Bay's Lambeau Field (below). **Photo courtesy the Green Bay Packers Hall of Fame Inc.**

One of the 1926 Eskimos and the star of the Kelley-Duluth team, West-Duluth native and Denfeld High grad Wally Gilbert was better known in the sporting world as the best third basemen to ever play for the Brooklyn Dodgers.
Photo courtesy the *Duluth News Tribune*.

A detail from a photo collage on display at the Packers Hall of Fame. **Photo courtesy Denis Gullickson.**

Ole Haugsrud, the Eskimos owner. Because of a promise by NFL officials made in 1929 when he sold the Eskimos, Haugsrud became part owner of the Minnesota Vikings in 1961—32 years later and about the time of this photo. He helped bring quarterback Fran Tarkenton to the Vikings.
Photo courtesy the *Duluth News Tribune*.

Ole Haugsrud (left) and former Eskimos player Bill Stein of Two Harbors, Minnesota, pack a trunk of memorabilia destined for Canton, Ohio, and the Pro Football Hall of Fame in 1962. Note the jersey in Stein's hands: the Eskimos were the first NFL team to sport a logo on their uniforms.
Photo courtesy the *Duluth News Tribune*.

The Eskimos' exhibit in the Pro Football Hall of Fame, featuring memorabilia provided by Haugsrud.
Photo courtesy the *Duluth News Tribune*.

Ernie Nevers in a punting pose while sporting his Eskimos uniform. Note the autograph—this is a reproduction of Eskimos owner Ole Haugsrud's personal copy. Nevers signed the photo: "To Ole Haugsrud, the truest friend and greatest fellow I ever met. Very Sincerely, 'Ernie' Nevers." Haugsrud and Nevers knew each other from their years at Superior, Wisconsin's Central High School and teamed up to create the 1926 Duluth Eskimos.
Photo courtesy Bob Murphy and Barry Singer.

Ernie Nevers (seated) and Bronislau "Bronko" Nagurski pose with a plaque the day both were inducted into the Duluth Hall of Fame. Nagurski, a legendary running back for the Chicago Bears and a world-champion professional wrestler, grew up in International Falls, Minnesota, north of Duluth. Both were charter members of the Professional Football Hall of Fame in 1963, along with former Eskimos back Johnny "Blood" McNally.
Photo courtesy the *Duluth News Tribune*.

Perhaps the purest "leatherhead" among the Eskimos—and certainly worthy of their "Iron Men of the North" nickname—Walt Kiesling spent his NFL career both in the trenches and on the sidelines. After his tenure with the Eskimos, the hall-of-famer from St. Paul played for Green Bay, the Chicago Cardinals, and the Chicago Bears. After his playing days he coached for the Pittsburgh Pirates and Steelers, taking on the head coaching mantle at least twice (he was also an assistant coach with Green Bay). Dick McCann, the Professional Football Hall of Fame's first director, said, "Walt Kiesling didn't just watch pro football grow from the rocky sandlots. He shoved it along the way. He was one of the game's truly remarkable pioneers."
Photo courtesy the Pittsburgh Steelers.

SIX

THE ESKIMOS
HIT THE ROAD

Nevers arrived in Two Harbors on the second day of training camp. He was "in splendid condition following a season as a pitcher with the St. Louis Browns," the *Duluth News Tribune* reported. "He will lose no time in whipping his Eskimos into shape." He took over "in his quiet, unassuming manner."

Within an hour, the All-American was in uniform, directing his team in drills and teaching them the offense he learned at Stanford University from coach "Pop" Warner. The offense revolved around the halfback, and for the Eskimos, more often than not, that meant Nevers. With his athleticism and knack for deception, he was ideally suited. The fullback took the snap from center and dictated the flow of every play. He was free to run the ball, hand it off to another runner, or give it to the quarterback for a pass down field. The offense was run from four patterns: single wing, double wing, I formation, and box formation.

An innovation Nevers introduced to his players was huddling before plays. Common now, but gathering an offensive team together prior to the snap of the ball to make sure everyone knew the play was something no teams did then. Generally, the halfback just got the ball and decided what to do with it, usually choosing to run.

Nevers wrapped up the afternoon drills by concentrating on the basics: kicking, passing, and rushing, or "charging," as running the football was often called then because of the way the ball carrier charged into the line, hoping to break through for a gain.

"Not a single grumble has been heard from members of the squad against the strict training grind adopted by Nevers and the management of the club in their effort to bring their squad to the peak of condition," Cubby Campbell wrote after the third day of training camp. Players told Campbell that Nevers was "a regular fellow [with a] thorough knowledge of the game. His emphatic yet easy manner in detailing points of a play and, above all, his winning personality has already won over the members of the team."

Their third night in Two Harbors, the Eskimos were honored guests at a dance at the Hotel Agate. The hotel's owner, Mrs. Kelly—or "Mother," as the players had already started calling her in appreciation of the bountiful feeds she prepared for them—hosted the occasion.

Practices the next day were called by Campbell the "stiffest workout of the week.... All the variations of grid work were performed." A "brisk" scrimmage was held in the afternoon.

After short signal drills and a workout with his team on the morning of Saturday, September 11, 1926, Nevers announced the players who'd participate in an exhibition game scheduled the following day in Superior, Wisconsin.

Lining up or taking turns in the backfield with Nevers against the Gogebic Panthers of Ironwood, Michigan—Johnny Blood McNally's former team—would be McNally, Doc Kelly, Russ Method, Cobb Rooney (in his third season in Duluth), Paul Fitzgibbon, and Arthur Charles "Red" Quam, a native of Minneapolis and a one-time member of the famous and rugged Quantico Marine football team. He found his way to Duluth via the reserve officers' training camp in Fort Eustis, Virginia.

The centers, Nevers said, would be Harry "Porky" Rundquist—a "stalwart lineman," according to Haugsrud—and Bill Stein, in his fourth season.

The guards on the lineup card were Doc Williams, also back in Duluth after three seasons with the Duluth-Kelley team; Hew Sullivan, a twenty-eight-year-old rookie from Chisholm, Minnesota; and Jimmy Manion of Jasper, Minnesota, a "small but fast guard," as Haugsrud called him, and a product of Minnesota's University of St. Thomas.

On the flank, Nevers said, were Jack Underwood, another third season veteran; Joe Rooney, back from the Rock Island Independents; and Oke Carlson.

The tackles included Art Johnson; Walter Edward "Chuck" or "Chet" Gayer of Janesville, Minnesota, a teammate of Fitzgibbon at Creighton; and Walter Kiesling, a rookie who had once been recruited to play for Notre Dame but who played instead for his hometown University of St. Thomas in St. Paul, Minnesota. The decision came at the urging of Kiesling's mother, who felt South Bend, Indiana, was just too far from home.

Kiesling, or the "Big Kies," launched a hall-of-fame football career with the 1926 Duluth Eskimos that would come to include thirteen stellar seasons of rough-and-tumble line play with six different franchises and twenty-three years of coaching in Pittsburgh for the Pirates and later the Steelers. Kiesling was "larger, stronger, and tougher than most of his opponents," the Pro Football Hall of Fame noted when Kiesling was inducted with the class of 1966.

~

The Eskimos' roster of eighteen—the "most powerful team in [Duluth's] history," as the *Duluth News Tribune* boasted—boarded a bus that carried it back down the Lake Superior shoreline from Two Harbors to Duluth. The night before the exhibition game, the players checked in to the West Duluth YMCA, a four-story brick structure at 605 North Central Avenue. (Today the building is the Memorial Park Apartments; the Young Men's Christian Association moved out its operations in 1960.)

The players, perhaps enjoying their freedom a bit too much after a week of hard work and rigid structure, didn't remain in their YMCA rooms for long.

"I got a call that night," Haugsrud recalled. The team owner was invited to move his players out. Immediately.

"It was an innocent mistake," Haugsrud reminisced. "The boys had somehow got the impression that there was a fire and they went out and got the fire hose and sprayed the halls and stairs.

"I had to move them all to the Superior YMCA."

~

The following morning the players prepared for battle, their first as the Duluth Eskimos.

They pulled on knee-high socks, long-sleeved jerseys decorated with igloos across their chests, and rugged, knee-length football trousers with extra padding at the knees, thighs, and elsewhere. They laced up leather, cleated, ankle-high athletic shoes, and they tucked their heads inside dog-eared leather football helmets.

Nevers added an extra bit of equipment: About ten yards of tape that he wrapped tightly around his once-broken and forever-weakened ankles. He started taping two hours before games, Haugsrud said.

On a perfect autumn afternoon, sunshine warmed the more than three thousand sports enthusiasts who filled Superior's Hislop Park for the Eskimos' debut against the Gogebic Panthers. The stadium—named for the late George Hislop, a sports fan, city alderman, and member of the Superior Board of Public Works—had been chosen over Duluth's Athletic Park because of its greater seating capacity, and it was filled to its limits. The throng included supporters from Michigan's Upper Peninsula who traveled west to Superior aboard a special train—and with a clown. The crowd, reportedly, was the largest to take in an athletic contest in the Head of the Lakes region up to that time.

"We drew three or four thousand at the box office," Haugsrud said in *The Game That Was*. "But there were just as many standing on the [nearby] boxcars, watching [for] free. The ballpark had railroad tracks on both sides. The railroad men would leave boxcars lined up all along there."

For four straight games in 1924 and 1925, Duluth's and Ironwood's pro teams had battled to scoreless ties. Late in the 1925 season, Kelley-Duluth had finally broken through, winning 9-0 in a game played in Ironwood. The latest meeting promised to be a good one.

And the Eskimos had reason to be optimistic. Their roster now featured three future hall-of-famers, one of them enjoying a homecoming of sorts. Nevers' Superior Central High School Vikings played home games at Hislop Park. In addition, the Eskimos' line, "from wing to wing, averaged well over 200 pounds while the backfield [also was] exceptionally heavy and speedy," as the *Duluth News Tribune* reported.

The ball was put into play at 3 P.M. by referee Art Von of Duluth, a former player and a veteran official; umpire Kenneth "Bunk" Harris, a former star back for Duluth Central High School and a member of the Kelley-Duluth team in 1923; and head linesman Carl Donich of Ironwood, a graduate of the University of Illinois.

The Eskimos' Cobb Rooney took the opening kick in the shadow of his own goal posts and scampered forty yards before being dragged to the turf. From there, Nevers crashed through holes created by Kiesling, Stein, and others.

Early in the opening quarter, a line plunge by Nevers put the Eskimos close to the Panthers' goal line. Wingback Doc Kelly "crashed over" the top of a block made by Kiesling and into the end zone for the game's first score. Method booted the extra point.

In the second quarter, Nevers squirmed through the right side of the line for four yards and Kelly hit the same hole for another four to put the ball three feet shy of the end zone. On the next play, Nevers "broke through like a battering wedge, twisting his body edgewise to break the staunch line the visitors had drawn up at the place of attack," Cubby Campbell reported. The touchdown made the score 13-0, which was what it remained when Method's attempt for the extra point failed.

After halftime, the Panthers finally got in position to score, but Nevers intercepted the pass. The third quarter remained scoreless. Early in the fourth, Nevers ran the ball three straight times and then plowed into the end zone to make the score 19-0. The Eskimos were pulling away. Duluth added one more touchdown later in the fourth quarter when Nevers leaped through a wide opening in the center of the line to the five-yard line. Hitting the same hole on the next play, he slipped into the end zone.

Nevers was a star—or was still a star. His running was "terrific" and "unstoppable," Campbell wrote. He averaged a little better than fifty yards on six punts, and he connected with Cobb Rooney on pass after pass, his golden arm proving as deadly on the gridiron in the fall as it had been all summer on the baseball diamond. Nevers even played stellar defense.

Another star of the game was Fitzgibbon who "won himself a firm place with the fans of the Twin Ports by his brilliant open-field running," Campbell wrote. "On the first play that he was given the ball, Fitz darted for the off-tackle play, but finding the way blocked, he circled wide on left end, shaking off several tacklers before being brought down at the end of a fifteen-yard gain."

The Eskimos' defense contributed, too, holding Gogebic to one first down all afternoon, "that by Joe Gotts, the sensational little quarterback from Ironwood who whirled around [right end] for a fifteeen-yard gain," as Campbell reported.

The huddle system was too slow, according to Campbell, allowing Gogebic "abundant time to get set for whatever play was coming," but the victory was thorough, and a sign of what was to come.

~

Training camp in Two Harbors, Minnesota. An exhibition game in Superior, Wisconsin. An NFL schedule completely and entirely void of home games. Where were the Duluth Eskimos?

More than a few fans were miffed and feeling pangs of abandonment as baseball season gave way to football that fall of 1926. The football faithful griped about their wanderlust NFL team. They talked about the obvious need to fix up old Athletic Park, and they made sure their displeasure was well known.

Meanwhile, two people went to work to address the dilemma and to remedy the ruckus. Haugsrud and Athletic Park promoter and manager Cub La Joy launched into days of intense negotiations to bring the Kansas City Cowboys, an NFL-designated road team like the Eskimos, to Duluth for the season opener. At one point, they reached an agreement: The September 19 game would be played at Hislop Park in Superior. The deal lasted about twenty-five hours. Following a final long-distance phone call, Haugsrud and La Joy announced the game would be played at Athletic Park. Duluth fans could rejoice. The deal even required the park's rickety grandstands to be fixed up and new sideline seats to be constructed.

"They nicked me for $500 in promoting this contest," La Joy complained, according to author Ross Bernstein. "But I'm hoping that the weatherman and the sports fans of the Twin Ports will pull me through on the sunny side."

Just three days before the contest, carpenters and contractors went to work to repair the wooden bleachers and grandstands. They quickly constructed eight hundred box seats along the sidelines. And they got the field as ready as it had ever been.

While hammers flew in Duluth, the Kansas City Cowboys began their journey north by train. They arrived in Minneapolis on Tuesday, September 14, and conducted drills the following day at the University of St. Thomas in St. Paul. On Thursday, September 16, the team arrived in Duluth for a workout at Athletic Park and another at Duluth Cathedral High School. They taught the high school players about technique and tactics and used them as a scout team for a scrimmage.

The Eskimos, meanwhile, practiced at Athletic Park and at the Blaine School field in Superior.

On Saturday, September 18, the Cowboys displayed the pizazz that led the NFL to designate the franchise a road team. In every town they visited, they rented horses and marched, in full regalia, to the stadium, with players from the other team participating as well. One march down Broadway Avenue in New York attracted upwards of fifty thousand spectators. In Duluth they marched along West Superior Street from downtown to the hastily renovated stadium. Duluthians ate it up.

~

The morning after the parade, the head coaches for the Eskimos and Cowboys issued statements about that afternoon's contest.

"This game means considerable to us," Eskimos manager Dewey Scanlon said. "Ernie Nevers will put all his resources on the field in an attempt to win the game—and by a comfortable score. With an array of powerful talent supporting him, Nevers is expected to be at his best this afternoon, and I'm confident we will win."

Cowboys coach Roy Andrews said, "I've got a line that will rope and tie up Mr. Nevers every time he attempts to gallop through our front wall. Nevers will be never more when we get through with him." He also had a counterpart for Nevers, halfback Al Bloodgood, a second year player and former college star for the University of Nebraska.

An estimated throng of six thousand fans—another Head of the Lakes record—packed every available seat and stood several deep around three sides of the playing field at Athletic Park.

"The game was slowly played," Cubby Campbell reported. "Numerous penalties and delays of various sorts [combined] to make the contest interesting and thrilling only in spots.... The game as a whole lacked continuous excitement."

The Cowboys "clearly outplayed" Duluth in the first quarter but weren't able to score.

The Eskimos came to life before halftime, driving deep into Cowboys territory. But it was all for naught when a place kick by Nevers sailed wide.

The Cowboys took over. A pair of line plunges gained little. A forward pass misfired. On fourth down, the Cowboys lined up for another pass, but "the Duluth forward wall swarmed through on the gray-haired K.C. veteran, [and Eskimos guard John T. "Jock"] Murray and Kiesling hitting him hard as he was about to hurl the ball. The pigskin fell from his hands and rolled toward the Cowboys goal. Kiesling attempted to recover but missed. Underwood, however, scooped up the rolling oval and raced easily over the goal line,

Nevers completing the scoring by [splitting the uprights] for the final point."
The Eskimos took the lead.

Nevers and the Eskimos dominated the rest of the quarter. Nevers gained ten or more yards on several runs. More than one of his punts sailed sixty yards or better. Other boots angled out of bounds, keeping the Cowboys pinned back on their own end of the field. Neither side scored.

In the second half, the "game was an extremely rough-and-tumble affair with a lot of skirmishes breaking out near the end," Bernstein wrote. "Nevers, who was retaliating for being choked, was even penalized 15 yards for unnecessary roughness on a 'slugging' call. The game came down to defense and field position with Nevers…proving to be the difference."

The Eskimos triumphed in their season opener, 7-0.

Then, with their mackinaw jackets and igloo-emblazoned jerseys, the team caught a train out of town. With the Eskimos out of town, Duluth football fanatics resumed their grumbling.

~

What's believed to be the longest road trip in sports history chugged away from a Duluth train station hours after the Eskimos dispatched the Kansas City Cowboys. Over the next 117 days, spanning from 1926 into 1927, and across seventeen thousand miles, the Eskimos would play thirteen additional league games and fifteen exhibitions.

They'd travel as far east as Portland, Maine, and as far west as San Francisco. They'd play five games in eight days at one point. And they'd do it with broken noses, broken fingers, torn muscles, and other maladies.

Sometimes some of them wouldn't be able to play to all. As few as two players at a time sometimes sat on the bench. And they weren't always players, either. The manager of the team and the team owner sometimes put on uniforms and occupied space on the sidelines in the hope that the opposition wouldn't notice their team was so short-handed.

The Duluth Eskimos would journey by train, by bus, and once by boat. Their traveling would be chaotic. *Sports Illustrated*'s Rick Reilly would joke decades later that the Eskimos were always in such a hurry the players had to hang their just-washed uniforms out their bus and train windows to dry. Ralph Hickok would report that the Eskimos took two showers after their games: one with their uniforms on to get off all the mud and another to get themselves clean.

A comment once made by Ernie Nevers confirmed that the reports maybe weren't so tongue-in-cheek: "We'd beat [our uniforms] like rugs to get some of the water out, throw them into our [trunks], get dressed, and catch a train. Hell, most of the time we were only half dressed when we boarded."

The road trip, from the moment it chugged away from Duluth to the moment it returned some five months and countless stories later, would become an ingrained part of NFL lore. It would become a big part of the reason Chicago Bears' owner George "Papa Bear" Halas would call the Eskimos "the greatest football team ever put together."

~

The Eskimos' first stop on their way to fame was a waterlogged City Stadium in Green Bay, Wisconsin, and a matchup with the Packers. A steady rain the morning of October 3, 1926, combined with a downpour just after the opening kick to soak more than three thousand fans while turning the playing surface into an ankle-deep pit of mud and standing water. The weather left the teams little choice but to play straight-ahead, smash-mouth football.

The first quarter was scoreless as both teams tried to run the ball on the slippery field. In the opening moments of the second quarter, however, the Packers, well known for their aerial attack, attempted a pass. Nevers picked off the errant throw at the Eskimos' twenty-yard line and then splashed some sixty-five yards unmolested down the sideline before being caught and downed by Packers' guard Moose Gardner.

Line smashes by Nevers, Paul Fitzgibbon, and Cobb Rooney moved the ball to the two-foot line, but no farther. The Packers' defense stiffened, and the score remained 0-0.

The two teams sloshed to near the end of the game when the Packers finally threatened. End runs and a pair of completed passes moved the ball to the Eskimos' twenty-yard line. But three running attempts from there, each into the middle of the line, gained little. And a drop kick failed to split the uprights.

Despite thrills from Nevers and sterling line play by the Eskimos' Bill Stein, Doc Williams, and Joe Rooney, according to the *Green Bay Press Gazette*'s coverage, the game ended in a soaking wet scoreless tie.

~

A week later, the Eskimos traveled south to Hammond, Indiana, near Gary, for an October 10 game against the Hammond Pros. The Pros were coming off a disappointing fourteenth-place finish in 1925.

Neither team scored in the opening quarter at Hammond Turner Field. Early in the second period, the Eskimos put together five straight first downs behind the precision passing of Nevers and the determined running of Cobb Rooney, Cuss Method, and Blood McNally. From the five-yard line, McNally got the call—and the ball—and punched into the end zone to give his team the lead.

In the third quarter Duluth moved the ball to the Hammond ten-yard line. The defense, looking for a line smash, was fooled when the Eskimos instead lobbed a pass over the line to Cobb Rooney. The lead was two touchdowns.

The Pros rallied, but a pass by Harry Curzon was intercepted by Method, who raced forty yards into the end zone, and the Eskimos moved ahead by three touchdowns.

Late in the game, Nevers mixed line smashes and razor-sharp passes for a handful of first downs and then took the ball in himself to make the final score 26-0.

~

The unbeaten Eskimos—who had yet give up a single point in 1926—took their show a hundred miles north of Hammond, along the Lake Michigan shoreline, to Racine, Wisconsin, where their first challenge wasn't on the grid-iron.

A speakeasy owner "who was extremely proud of his German shepherd's springing ability…was so confident that his hound was the fastest thing on four legs that he was willing to place a wager on any member of the Eskimos team who thought he could beat the mongrel in a race," as Ross Bernstein would later write.

The players scraped together $75 and nominated Blood McNally, their ready-for-anything halfback, to take on the canine. McNally pounded back a couple of drinks to take off an edge that was rarely visible and then calmly went out back to share a start line with a canine.

"Blood won handily," football historian Ralph Hickok reported. "The Eskimos collected their winnings and sportingly offered the speakeasy owner a chance to get his money back on the football game. He accepted."

The next challenge came from the Racine Tornadoes, back in the NFL after a year's hiatus. Some 2,600 fans, including one very interested speakeasy operator, filled Racine's Horlick Field for the Sunday, October 17, 1926, matchup.

The opening period was scoreless for both teams. In the second quarter, Nevers shot a thirty-four-yard pass to Blood McNally, who plunged into the end zone. On their next possession, Nevers hit Method through the air for thirty-five yards to move the ball to the Racine ten-yard line. Nevers then faked a pass to one side, spun, and fired to McNally on the other side for a touchdown and a 14-0 lead.

In the third quarter, a bad punt by Racine's Wally McIllwain, playing his only season in the NFL, gave the Eskimos the ball at the Tornadoes' fifteen. Nevers and Fitzgibbon plunged into and through the linemen to move the ball close to the goal line. Then Fitzgibbon took it in for the score to wrap up the 21-0 final.

Back at the speakeasy, the Eskimos were able to collect again.

~

The following Sunday, the undefeated, first-place Eskimos faced the Chicago Bears at rowdy Wrigley Field. An estimated crowd of twelve thousand filled the stands, many of them to see the Eskimos' Nevers.

The only scoring in the first half was a twenty-five-yard field goal by future hall-of-famer Paddy Driscoll. The Eskimos had finally given up a score, and were behind by three points.

A mix of passes and runs on the Bears' opening drive of the second half took the ball all the way to the Eskimos seven-yard line. Milt Romney crashed through the Duluth defensive line from there to give his team a 10-0 margin. When the Bears got the ball back they went right back to work. Bill Senn scooted his lanky, six foot, 177-pound frame around end and broke loose for a sixty-eight-yard gain to the Eskimos' twelve-yard line. A Driscoll pass to Oscar Knop was deflected by two Eskimos, but somehow the eight-year veteran was able to hold on, falling at the Duluth one-foot line. Senn plunged in from there. Before the third quarter was over, the Bears turned a series of skillful and successful forward passes into their third touchdown of the quarter.

The Eskimos lit up the scoreboard in the final quarter with line plunges by Nevers, finishing up with one into the end zone from three yards out. But it wasn't enough. The Eskimos avoided the shutout, but dropped their first game of the season, 24-6.

SEVEN

UNDER THE LIMIT

Win or lose, the Eskimos were quickly learning how to rely on each other to survive the grind of the open road.

"There were no prima donas on this ball club," Haugsrud wrote nearly four decades later. "Every man packed his own bag."

And played other very specific roles, as well.

Bill Stein, the center, was responsible for all suits and baggage. "We didn't have equipment men, trainers, and the rest like they do today," Stein said in a 1963 interview. He made "sure we got our equipment to the next place we played.

"I don't ever remember anyone missing a game because we forgot his gear," Stein said. "The worst, I guess, [came] after playing a game in the rain. Some of the boys laid their equipment out next to [a] boiler to dry. The next day the shoes were all warped out of shape."

Russ Method, at back, served as team trainer. Haugsrud did what he did best: publicity. He also answered correspondence, organized daily schedules, booked transportation and hotels, and managed all finances. Three players handled radio interviews and after-dinner speaking engagements: Blood McNally, Doc Williams, and Nevers, who once said of the team's never-ending road trip, "This must be the most exciting period in all history."

McNally also entertained his teammates. "The long train rides seemed the shorter because of Johnny Blood," Nevers once said. "He had so many interests and was always doing something that excited the Eskimos. They even liked his dramatic recitations and his singing. He was around twenty-two then but he was just a kid at heart. It would be hard to imagine us going through that long season without Johnny Blood. His amazing stunts did so much to lighten the pressure and drudgery."

With every player assuming a role, the Eskimos and their camaraderie hummed as smoothly off the field as on it.

~

A diagnosis of appendicitis prompted doctors to order Nevers to the sidelines for the Eskimos' next game, a Halloween afternoon date with the Milwaukee Badgers at Milwaukee Athletic Park.

With their star out of the lineup, the Eskimos held their own, but barely, through a scoreless first half. After the intermission, Nevers defied his doctors' orders and decided to enter the game.

"What else could I do? I had to put myself into the game," he said, practically apologizing for his recklessness, as reported by Arthur Daley of the *New York Times*. "So I played the rest of the way."

Dropping back from his own twenty-yard line, Nevers, nowhere near full strength, let fly a long pass that badly missed the intended receiver. The Badgers' Duke Slater picked it off and raced for a touchdown and a 6-0 third-quarter advantage. The extra point failed, but the lead held up.

With the game clock ticking down from the five-minute mark, Duluth took the ball on its own twenty-five-yard line. Rush after rush, most of them by Nevers, tallied five straight first downs as the Eskimos moved the ball down field. With only two minutes left, Nevers dropped back and hurled a thirty-five-yarder into the end zone to teammate Joe Rooney, tying the game. Nevers' kick for the extra point gave his Eskimos their fourth league victory.

A newspaper writer in Milwaukee couldn't help but gush about Nevers, who was more than living up to his hype: "Ernie Nevers proved to a handful of pro football fans here today why he was chosen All-American fullback last fall and why ol' Pop Warner, Stanford coach, called him the greatest football player he ever saw, for Ernie personally led his Duluth Eskimos to a 7-6 victory over Johnny Bryan's Badgers, earned almost solely by his own efforts."

~

Perhaps still sore, or perhaps heeding at least some of his doctors' good advice, Nevers deferred running and ball-handling duties to several teammates throughout much of a November 7 matchup with the Detroit Panthers at Detroit Navin Field in Michigan.

A defensive battle played in front of a record twenty-one thousand fans, including about nine thousand newsboys who were treated to the game by the team and by Detroit newspapers. The score stood at 0-0 when Nevers finally took the ball in the third period. He quickly racked up fifty-seven yards and would finish with six first downs on the day, but he wasn't able to punch the ball into the end zone. Nor was he able to get the ball close enough for a makable field goal. Nevers missed four boots on the day, all from long distance. The tries included a fifty-one-yarder with time running out that fell just inches short.

Detroit blew three field goal tries of its own, the first two when Eddie Scharer failed to get the ball into position and the third when Gus Sonnenberg missed the mark from forty-five yards away.

The Eskimos consistently stuffed the plunges and running of Detroit's Phil Marion. The high point for the Duluth eleven was a sixty-yard punt by Nevers. "Even the hostile Detroit fans gave him a hero's hand," the *Detroit Free Press* reported. "Although both teams played with their utmost strength, neither could pierce the other's stubborn defense for a touchdown."

The game ended in a scoreless tie, yet, the newspaper said, was "one of the hardest fought and cleanest professional football games ever seen in Detroit."

Not entirely clean, according to Haugsrud, who recounted a story from the game that showed why professional football in the 1920s was regarded much as professional wrestling is today:

> [The Panthers'] Gus Sonnenberg, world heavyweight champion wrestler, was playing in the line opposite Doc Williams. Gus [looked] Williams… up and down for defects and decided Doc's ankles were vulnerable. Promptly he crashed into one of them, nearly breaking it.

> "You try that trick again and we're both going out of the game," Doc warned him. Shortly afterward, Gus dove toward William's other ankle. Doc sidestepped, grabbed Sonnenberg by the seat of the pants with one hand and the back of the neck with the other. Raising the squirming champion high in the air, [he] crashed him head foremost against the frozen turf. The officials sent both players to the showers.

~

Most teams in the NFL boasted rosters of twenty-two men, the maximum allowed by the 1926 rules. Duluth had started the season with eighteen, and been down to sixteen before the Detroit game. With a pair of injuries in that game, the Eskimos limped into New York with only fourteen players for its Thursday, November 11, game against the Giants at the Polo Grounds.

"Naturally, we felt somewhat abashed with [so few] substitutes to hold down the bench," Haugsrud wrote. "To relieve this, Coach [Dewey] Scanlon and I would also appear in moleskins and participate in the warm-up practice before contests. I usually went through the motions of drop kicking and, when the whistle blew, scurried for the bench where I remained until they called for the water boy."

Upon arriving in New York via ferry from Providence, Rhode Island, the Eskimos were pleasantly surprised when Giants' owner Tim Mara rolled up to their hotel with a large sightseeing bus. Haugsrud told football historian Ralph Hickok:

> "[Mara] invited us to hop in and see the Metropolis at his expense. This was a much-appreciated gesture and we climbed into the conveyance— all fifteen of us. Still, the bus didn't start.
>
> Finally, after considerable delay, Mara says, "Tell the rest of your players to hurry and get in, we have to get under way." I explained the other boys were tired of riding and desired to rest in their rooms. "Very well," he agreed. "Let's go."
>
> I didn't want him to know this was the whole team.

Realizing later that Haugsrud and his fourteen players were indeed the entire Eskimos squad, Mara balked at their small ranks. This is "a football team?" he asked in amazement.

Famed New York sportswriter Grantland Rice quickly answered the Giants owner, his response dubbing the Eskimos with the nickname that follows them to this day: "That's the Iron Men of the North," Rice said.

~

Just four days after playing in Detroit, the Eskimos' limited lineup took the field in New York. Temperatures hovered at a bone-chilling twenty degrees as some five thousand fans jammed into the Polo Grounds.

New York took the opening kick and drove straight down the field behind the ball carrying of Jack McBride. He capped the drive by diving across the goal line and kicking the extra point for an early 7-0 lead.

The Eskimos came right back, marching down the field in similar fashion. The drive was highlighted by a beautiful forty-yard pass from Ernie Nevers to Cobb Rooney. Finally, Nevers plunged into the end zone from two yards out and added the extra point to knot the game at seven points apiece. Both teams' defenses then settled in. The remainder of the opening half was scoreless.

The third quarter brought a scary moment for the Duluth eleven when Nevers was kicked in the head and knocked unconscious.

With their star on the sidelines, the Eskimos fumbled at midfield and then allowed Giants' runner Hinkey Haines to break into the open field and race for a twenty-five-yard touchdown. McBride added another extra point, and the New Yorkers were up 14-7.

Nevers managed to collect himself and return to the game in the fourth quarter, almost certainly another ill-advised move, medically speaking. With time running down and the ball on his team's own twenty-yard line, Nevers ran for six straight first downs. The drive included nine consecutive rushes for fifty-five yards—and a touchdown that trimmed the lead to 14-13.

The shorthanded Iron Men could tie with the extra point.

But on the attempt, the Giants' Walter Clarence "Tilly" Voss, a seven-year veteran, beat his man off the ball and was able to race in from his end position. He hurled himself through the air and blocked Nevers' kick, preserving the Giants' thrilling, hard-fought victory.

"Following the game, the huge crowd of fans…surged out on the field and gave Nevers an ovation which was probably as sincere and as enthusiastic as he ever received at his alma mater on the West Coast," *Duluth News Tribune* correspondent Bud Rennie wrote. "The big blond star surely deserved the tribute, for he was by far the most thrilling personage ever witnessed in action in Gotham…. Without him the game would have been uninteresting."

The Giants' Steve Owen piled on the praise: "I was wondering where Nevers was hurt," he said, according to Ross Bernstein. "It could only have been his big toe."

~

The Eskimos were forced to quickly shake off the difficult loss in New York. They had another game just two nights later in Philadelphia against the Frankford Yellow Jackets, a team surging toward an NFL championship. A rowdy crowd of six thousand filled Frankford Stadium to see the talents of Duluth's Ernie Nevers.

The Yellow Jackets scored first when nine-year veteran Adolph Frederick "Swede" Youngstrom picked off an Eskimos pass and raced it into the end zone in the opening quarter. Rookie John Walter Budd added the extra point.

At the end of the opening half, the Eskimos drove to the Frankford one-yard line. They were looking to knot the game at seven going into halftime. But the clock ran out before they could push the ball across.

In the third quarter, Johnny Budd added a field goal, and the Yellow Jackets had the win, a shutout, 10-0.

~

The Eskimos, still shorthanded—and smarting after two straight losses—hurried to get back on the road. Immediately following the Frankford contest, they traveled about a hundred miles to Pottsville, "a mining city in the Pennsylvania coal hills where they enjoy Sunday sports contrary to the state law," as Haugsrud described the place. A game against the Pottsville Maroons was scheduled the very next day.

Rather than turning in for the good night's sleep they certainly needed, Blood McNally, Walt Kiesling, and Cobb Rooney found a local speakeasy. It was located in a firehouse. Well lubricated, Rooney and McNally got to talking about which one of them would win in a fistfight. The talk turned into a friendly argument and the friendly argument eventually continued outside in the alley where the men decided they'd find out. Kiesling agreed to referee. The first punch that landed, a big roundhouse right hook, was thrown by McNally. But rather than hitting Rooney, McNally's fist smacked square into a brick wall.

The next morning the trio told Haugsrud how McNally had managed to break his hand. Haugsrud was furious.

"I fired all three of them," he said, according to several sources. "But that was in the morning. Well, I knew I needed them for the game, so I hired them back at noontime. Kies and Johnny are both in the Hall of Fame. I'm probably the only manager who ever fired two hall of famers in one day."

Arriving at Minersville Park prior to the game, the Eskimos couldn't believe their eyes. "The whole damn [Pottsville] fire department was soaking the field with water," Nevers recalled, according to Hickok. "I guess they figured the only way they could beat us was to slow us down."

The strategy appeared effective through a scoreless first half that was made more bleak for Duluth when Nevers was knocked unconscious for the second time in three games. Yet again, however, he returned to play after halftime.

The second-half kickoff was returned by the Maroons' Jesse Brown seventy yards to the Duluth twenty. Several line smashes gained only about five yards, but then a pass from Brown, a southpaw, found six-foot end Charlie Berry at the three-yard line. Three plays later, Barney Wentz crashed over for the first score of the game, according to the *Pottsville Republican*. Coverage in the *Duluth News Tribune* indicated Brown was the one who slid over for the score. Either way, Jim Welsh added the extra point and the Maroons owned a 7-0 advantage.

Trying desperately to get back into the game, Nevers, at one point, completed seventeen straight passes, including several to Blood McNally, who was even able to pull in spectacular one-handed grabs. But the third quarter was scoreless for both teams.

In the final quarter, Nevers dropped back into his own end zone for a punt when the ball, made slippery by the still-wet field, squirted through his outstretched hands. Pottsville tackle Frankie Racis fell on the oval in the end zone for a 13-0 lead.

And for the victory.

Nevers' fumble was far from the Eskimos' only frustration on the afternoon, according to an oft-repeated account of the game that wasn't published in the following morning's Pottsville or Duluth newspapers.

The referees, umpires, head linesman, and field judge, Haugsrud wrote years later, were all "homers." They were "paid by the home team" and they gave Duluth a "disquieting afternoon":

> Time after time Duluth would get into scoring position only to be penalized anywhere from 10 to 50 yards for some trumped-up rule violation. Toward the end of the game, the Eskimos became exasperated. Captain Nevers felt the pressure of the gathering storm and admonished his players if they pulled any skull cracking or mayhem they might be thrown out of the league. On the next play, Duluth advanced the ball to the Pottsville five-yard line with first down coming up. Promptly, Duluth was penalized fifty yards.
>
> About this time, Bill Stein, who was about the most cool-headed player on the club, said, "This is the payoff." On the next play, Method, one of the hardest blockers in the league, crashed into the referee, knocking the latter giddy. Stein, Williams, Rooney, Underwood, and Johnson went into action with elbows high and swinging, and five Pottsville players

were carried to the sidelines. Jimmy Manion, our midget back [at five feet ten inches tall and 178 pounds], had a perfectly developed specialty in which he hurled himself through the air and then threw his feet at his adversary. Jimmy's feet caught the umpire in the mouth and drove out more teeth than a blacksmith-wristed dentist could pull in half an hour. Exit Mr. Umpire. The head linesman was the only one left with a whistle. He quickly blew same and called [the] game off.

Manion's referee-neutralizing tactic was oft-used by Duluth, the late Barry Singer, a Superior librarian and historian, wrote in 1986. But Singer described the tactic as a team effort: "At times when the team thought they were being penalized unfairly by the officials, they brought in Jimmy Manion, a midget back, and hurled him into the air in the direction of the umps to make a point. Football was more primitive then."

~

The East Coast swing had been a rough one. The Eskimos lost several players to injuries and were suiting up only fourteen men. Nevers lost consciousness twice, while McNally lost the feeling in his right hand. They had arrived in the Big Apple with a stellar 4-1-2 win-loss-tie record, but left Pennsylvania at 4-4-2. Worst of all, according to Haugsrud's recollections, the players had lost their cool during a game. A November 6 exhibition game with the St. Louis Gunners, the Eskimos hoped, could right their ship.

Haugsrud and Scanlon continued to suit up and warm up before games to give the appearance of a strong and healthy team. Haugsrud's drop kicks were even improving with all the extra work. "Sometime we'll let you kick the extra point, Ole," Nevers teased, according to Bernstein.

Haugsrud certainly was open to the idea. Pre-game warmups weren't the only times he was spending practicing, as he related in *The Game That Was*:

> In those days you didn't have the money to hire bands and marching units and things like that to entertain the crowd. So what we would do, sometimes before the game and sometimes at the half, was put on kicking exhibitions. We'd put Nevers and Blood and Russ Method and Walt Gilbert out there kicking, and I'd always stand about halfway to the goalposts and relay the ball back. I liked to drop kick myself. In fact, I kicked with either foot so once in a while I'd catch the ball from the fellows behind the goal posts and make a kick. You know, from the twenty-yard line, just for the fun of it.

I would often say to Ernie Nevers, "When we run up a big lead, why don't you put me in to kick?" But Ernie would say, "You'll get hurt, Swede."

The Eskimos ran up such a lead against the Gunners. The lead was 48-0—or 52-0, depending on which account you consider more accurate—and the ball was at the St. Louis thirty-yard line. "Nevers called me from the bench for a drop-kick," Haugsrud recalled.

Had Nevers had a change of heart? Haugsrud's big chance to play in a real game had arrived. He sprinted in from the sidelines. What he didn't realize was that center Bill Stein and the rest of the Eskimos had clued-in the Gunners.

"I held out my hands to receive the ball, the Duluth line opened, and about eight St. Louis men came thundering through, knocking me for a loop," Haugsrud recalled. "I got the joke. I'd been framed. I never did see the ball."

Haugsrud was steamed, but he'd get the last laugh.

"After the game they all came around for their paychecks," he said decades later in an interview with *Duluth News Tribune* sports columnist Bruce Bennett. "But I had my right hand swathed in bandages and told them, 'I'm sorry boys but that drop kick play of yours backfired. I think I have a broken hand and can't sign your checks.' You should have heard them howl then."

Another of Haugsrud's responsibilities on the road was collecting the Eskimos' guaranteed appearance fee from the home team as well their share of gate receipts. Haugsrud always tried to do this around halftime, he said. This helped avoid being cheated after the game was over. By collecting at the half, if he was short changed, he could pull his team off the field—or threaten to do so.

"The manager of the Gunners came up to me on the sidelines and handed me a check for better than $3,000, which was our guarantee," Haugsrud said in *The Game That Was*. "He walked away before I realized he hadn't paid me an additional $70 that he owed us to cover an expense item. I hollered to him but he knew what was on and started running. I chased him right across the football field and up the steps of the grandstand and across an open causeway. Then he ran into the ladies' room."

An usher at the door stopped Haugsrud.

"You can't go in there," the usher said.

"I'm going in," Haugsrud replied. And did.

"I cornered the fellow in a toilet and he gave me the seventy bucks."

~

From St. Louis, the Eskimos traveled to Ohio for exhibitions in Cleveland and Akron and for a league game against the Canton Bulldogs.

In Cleveland, the team stayed at the Allerton Hotel, a "kind of show business hotel," Haugsrud said, according to Bernstein. "The Marx Brothers and Mack Sennett's Bathing Beauties were there at the same time we were."

Hotel management had very strict rules when it came to matters of the heart. Women were allowed only on even-numbered floors and men only on odd-numbered floors.

"This was just the kind of silly rule the mischievous Blood loved to break," Haugsrud said.

Not long after the team checked in, Blood McNally strutted into an elevator. He handed the elevator attendant some change and asked her if she would please buy him some cigarettes. When she went over to the cigar stand, McNally commandeered her elevator.

"Of course, he didn't stop at a men's floor," Haugsrud said.

"The ensuing chase would have done credit to the Marx Brothers," Ralph Hickok recounted. "Haugsrud and Nevers went running up and down stairs, trying to catch the elevator. They finally corralled Blood on a fire escape and took him to his room."

On the team's second night in Cleveland, the players attended a dance in the hotel ballroom. Cobb Rooney, whose spirit was nearly as wild as that of his buddy Blood, found himself attracted to a good-looking blonde. He talked to her all evening and grew so infatuated he finally propositioned her, the hotel's rules be damned.

"She turned out to be Harpo Marx—in drag," Hickok reported.

EIGHT

END OF THE ROAD

Turning their attentions back to football, the 4-4-2 Eskimos lined up for a league game on November 21 against Jim Thorpe and the Canton Bulldogs.

The Eskimos started fast at Canton's Lakeside Park. A twenty-five-yard end run by Paul Fitzgibbon highlighted a better than fifty-yard drive in the opening quarter. Nevers and Cobb Rooney also had good gainers before Nevers crashed into the end zone from three yards out.

Before the quarter ended, Nevers added a twelve-yard field goal from a difficult angle, and the Eskimos led 10-0.

In the second quarter, Canton's defense pushed the Eskimos around a bit. Pinned back near their own goal line after a fifteen-yard penalty, the Eskimos were forced to punt. The Bulldogs' "Fats" Heny, all five feet eleven inches and 245 pounds of him, rushed in and blocked the boot. The ball rolled out of the back of the end zone, and Canton was awarded its first two points of the game.

They'd also be its last points. Duluth's defense, led by the line play of Doc Williams and Joe Rooney, held the home team to a mere two first downs. Duluth won going away—the Eskimos were two yards from the end zone when the final gun sounded—10-2.

Nevers didn't remember the game for his stellar play or the much-needed notch in the win column, but instead for a wallop he took from Thorpe. The hard tackle came on a punt fielded by Nevers. "I felt as though I was being pile-driven into the ground," he said, according to author Bernstein. "I've never been hit so hard before or since."

Was it possible Thorpe, the former star, had grown weary of all the hype over Nevers, the league's new star? Maybe he'd heard one too many times the comments of their one-time college coach, Pop Warner, who said Nevers was better than Thorpe because he played harder. Perhaps Thorpe was sending a message. If so, he certainly caught the attention of Nevers.

～

A Thanksgiving Day exhibition game in Buffalo was next on the docket for the Eskimos. The game was expected to be a tough one, and Nevers and Haugsrud were eager to see their players in bed early, resting.

"A light snow was falling [and] Blood, as usual, was missing," Nevers said in Jim Scott's *Ernie Nevers: Football Hero*:

> Looking out the window of our hotel, I saw him reading from a book to a crowd across the street. Ole went after him. It turned out Johnny was reading poetry. He escorted Blood back to his room on the sixth floor. He took away all his clothes except his shorts and locked the door from the outside. It was like trying to keep a tot in a playpen. It was easy for Johnny to shinny down the sides of the building to resume his oratory. Yes, he was back at it ten minutes later before the crowd could disperse. Since it meant that much to him, I didn't interfere again. But he must have gotten awfully cold in just his shorts to protect him from the snow.

～

The Eskimos' league schedule continued on November 27 with a tilt in Hartford, Connecticut, against the Hartford Blues. The Velodrome, a bicycle track in East Hartford that seated about eight thousand, filled with fans for the Saturday matinée.

In the first quarter, Nevers connected on a field goal from forty-one yards out. In the third quarter, he split the uprights two more times, the first from forty-three yards and the second from twenty-five. In the final quarter, Nevers carried the ball on three straight plays, crashed into the end zone, and added the extra point to account for all of his team's scoring, earning a 16-0 shutout.

"The crowd went wild," the Connecticut sportswriters crooned. "Fans here acclaimed Nevers as the greatest grid player ever seen in action here because of his outstanding performance…. [his] passing was perfect. [He threw] the ball with a deadly aim and with bullet-like speed." Nevers connected eleven times, many of them to Cobb Rooney.

The perfect compliment to Nevers' brilliance on offense was the Eskimos' "stonewall" defense, especially its linemen.

It was the Eskimos' fifth NFL win and their sixth shutout for the season.

～

The following day, Sunday, the Eskimos faced the Steam Roller at the Cycle-drome in Providence, Rhode Island.

The Eskimos piled up sixteen first downs and Nevers completed nine of seventeen pass attempts, six of them to Wally Gilbert. In all, Duluth connected on fourteen pass attempts. Nevers also recorded one interception.

But penalties stalled drive after drive for the Eskimos. Four Duluth players hobbled or had to be helped off the field because of injuries: Cobb Rooney, Russ Method, Paul Fitzgibbon, and Jimmy Manion. And the normally sure-footed Nevers missed on four field goal attempts, from twenty-one, thirty-one, thirty-five, and fifty yards. The fifty-yard drop kick actually came the closest, sailing just under the cross bar.

Luckily, the Duluth defense stepped up once again, limiting the home team to two first downs and only three completed passes. The game ended without either team scoring.

～

After the Providence game, Haugsrud received an alarming telegram from the team's bank in Duluth: "OLE YOU BETTER GET THOSE ESKIMOS HOME WHILE YOU STILL GOT ENOUGH BLUBBER MEAT TO FEED THEM."

After each game, Haugsrud had been sending a check to the bank. "And as we traveled," Haugsrud said, according to Bernstein, "I would write checks on our account…. It turned out that our checking account was about dry. What happened was that we had been paid $4,000 in New Britain, Connecticut, but when the Duluth bank put the check through it bounced. And we had gotten $3,000 in Hartford, but that check also got kicked in the tail."

The following morning at breakfast, Haugsrud called his team together and explained the telegram.

Cobb Rooney immediately jumped to his feet: "Ole, tell that banker to stick that telegram up his you-know-where. You just pay us fifteen bucks a week to eat on and pay our room rent and our transportation."

"Amen!" chimed in the rest of the team. "You can pay us our salary when you catch up."

"So we kept going," Haugsrud said in *The Game That Was*. "But actually there was something I could do about those rubber checks. Every club had to put up $5,000 with the league to cover this kind of situation, and the rule was that when a club was putting out bum checks, why, the first ones who got in there with their claim got the money. And that year we happened to be first. So we got our money back, and in two weeks all the boys were paid off."

~

After an exhibition in Brooklyn, the Eskimos wrapped up their league schedule with a rematch against the Kansas City Cowboys. The Cowboys' Al Bloodgood, a former University of Nebraska star, put the home team on the scoreboard first. He hit a field goal—from either fifteen yards out, as the *Kansas City Star* reported, or from thirty-five yards away, as the *Duluth News Tribune* said in its report—after teammate Milt Rehnquist recovered a Nevers' fumble deep in Eskimos' territory.

In the second quarter, the Cowboys added three more points after another Duluth fumble, this one at its own twenty-three yard line. Bloodgood split the uprights from either twenty-three yards away, as the Kansas City paper said, or from thirty-two yards, according to the *News Tribune*.

A short punt by the Eskimos' Wally Gilbert in the third quarter set up Bloodgood for a third time and a 9-0 Kansas City lead at the end of the half.

Duluth finally answered later in the third quarter. Led by Blood McNally, the Eskimos drove to their opponent's two-yard line, the key play a pass from Nevers to McNally. Kansas City staged a gutty goal-line stand, but Nevers finally cashed in with a plunge into the end zone. He added the extra point with a drop kick to put his Eskimos only two points behind at 9-7.

Playing desperately in the final quarter to overcome the slim deficit, the Eskimos perhaps pressed a bit too much. Nevers threw two interceptions, one of them setting up Bloodgood for a fourth field goal, this one from thirty yards.

The game ended with the Eskimos on the short end of a narrow 12-7 decision.

~

With a record of six wins, five losses, and three ties, Duluth finished the 1926 season in eighth place in the twenty-two-team NFL. At the end of November, the Bears were undefeated and in first place with eleven wins and two ties, the Frankford Yellow Jackets had lost only once with twelve wins and a tie, and the Pottsville Maroons had a record of ten wins, one loss, and one tie.

On December 4, the Bears and Yellow Jackets squared off, battling to a scoreless tie through three quarters and all but five minutes of the fourth. That's when the Bears broke through and reached the end zone, but Frankford blocked the extra point. The Yellow Jackets then marched down the field, scored a touchdown, and successfully converted the extra point for a 7-6 victory.

The next weekend, Frankford wrapped up the league championship by defeating the Providence Steam Roller. The Bears' 9-7 win on the same weekend over the Pottsville Maroons, whose defense had recorded ten shutouts in twelve games, proved meaningless. Nevertheless, the champion Yellow Jackets continued to struggle financially. Their crosstown AFL rivals, the Philadelphia Quakers, consistently outdrew them for fans en route to the AFL championship. And Frankford was far from the only NFL team to find hard times.

The New York Giants, despite picking up star tackle Steve Owen from the Kansas City Cowboys, lost $40,000 on the season in the face of competition from Grange, Pyle, and the New York Yankees. The readmitted Racine Tornadoes played only five games, winning just one of them, before running out of money and calling it quits once again. The Canton Bulldogs, even with the return of Jim Thorpe, finished the season flat broke and in twentieth place, with just one win against nine losses and three ties. The team disbanded. The league canceled its franchise.

Overall, the season was even worse for the startup AFL. In the end, the AFL had probably thrown around a little too much cash a little too quickly. The new league likely also underestimated fan loyalty in established NFL markets; the success of the Quakers' competition with the Yellow Jackets was the exception, not the rule. And a rash of foul weather that kept away fans didn't help either. AFL franchises folded one by one, and by December only a couple of AFL teams still existed. One of those, the Brooklyn Horsemen, was in serious financial trouble. The club's owner, a boxing promoter, decided he had to sell. Waiting to buy was Giants owner Tim Mara. Mara allowed the Horsemen to go dormant until the rest of the AFL followed suit.

～

Amid the misery of a struggling—but still surviving—NFL, one story emerged that helped to buoy the league while capturing the imaginations of a nation. The Eskimos' seventeen-thousand-mile, September-to-February road trip was a story for the ages; they may have fallen short of their championsip goals, but that didn't mean they stopped playing.

Right after his team's loss to the Cowboys in Kansas City, Haugsrud announced the Eskimos would depart immediately for exhibitions on the West Coast. Nevers had been a standout for California's Stanford University, and Haugsrud banked on his star's lingering drawing power to pack stadiums up and down the Pacific coastline. He was right. With Nevers being treated like a folk hero, Duluth scheduled at least ten exhibitions during a barnstorming tour that took them up and down the Golden State.

In Sacramento, fullback, halfback, and quarterback Cobb Rooney was forced to leave a game when he was kicked above the nose and "went to the hospital with his eyeball laying out on his cheek," Haugsrud recalled in *The Game That Was*.

"Before the squad was to leave [Sacramento] for San Francisco, where we were to play our next game, I inquired...as to Rooney's condition," Haugsrud wrote in 1963. Surgeons had saved Rooney's eye, but "the superintendent in charge informed me that Mr. Rooney would have to be hospitalized for a week. Two days later the superintendent called me [at my hotel in San Francisco] to inform me that Rooney had left the hospital without permission—and that was not all. The special nurse that had been taking care of Rooney could not be accounted for. I no more than hung up the receiver and in walked Cobb and a beautiful lady."

Rooney, his head bandaged, greeted his coach. "I want to introduce you to my future wife," he said. The two had run away together. Rooney played the exhibition game in San Francisco, and just days afterward he was married and his season was over.

In San Francisco, Johnny Blood McNally visited a Chinese museum, according to Haugsrud. "Blood came home with a wealth of material which he whipped into a story that sold for several hundred dollars" to a magazine.

On another night, McNally and a teammate took two young women out for dinner.

"After the feast they went to a cab stand," Haugsrud recalled. "There was a taxi there but no driver. Blood piled his party into the cab, delivered the girls to [their] respective homes and returned to the cab stand. There was still no one around so [he and his teammate] pinned a dollar to the steering wheel and sauntered home."

In Los Angeles, team manager Dewey Scanlon was called upon to sub for an injured halfback. In his hurry to get on the field, he grabbed the wrong leather helmet. Two plays later, the headgear, which was far too small, went flying. In the pileup at the end of the play, the spiked boot of a player named Brick Mueller "carved a semi-circle on Scanlon's head," Haugsrud wrote. "The medico who attended Dewey wrapped yards of white gauze around [his] head, and the squad christened him 'the Turk.'" The nickname was in reference to a famous 18th-century fraud, a mechanical chess-playing machine featuring a turban-clad automaton and a hidden, human operator.

～

The Eskimos returned to Duluth on February 5, 1927, "smiling" and with $4,000 in the bank, Haugsrud reported. That profit was especially noteworthy because the team had been as much as $6,000 to $7,000 in the hole during the road trip.

Barnstorming the West Coast following its completion of the league schedule proved particularly profitable for the Eskimos. Although the players had signed contracts promising to pay them $50 for games they lost, $60 for games they tied, and $75 for victories, the season went so well Haugsrud decided to pay every player $75 per game, no matter what the outcome.

Nevers earned more, of course. His base salary of $15,000 plus his share of gate receipts totaled more than $65,000 for the season. That's about $725,000 in today's dollars. He was "the highest ever paid in football" up to that point, Haugsrud claimed. Of his guaranteed $15,000 a year, Nevers once joked, according to the Pro Football Hall of Fame: "The only mistake I made was that I forgot to ask how long the season was going to be."

Not that Nevers didn't earn his money. "I can never forget the stellar performance which Nevers put on in every game on our memorable cross-country jaunt," Haugsrud wrote. "I agree with Coach Glenn Warner that Nevers is the greatest all-around backfield man that ever graced the gridiron." He captained the team, called all the signals, and did the majority of passing, punting, and place kicking. He was constantly on the field. On offense, on defense, for kicking plays, and even after suffering concussions. He reportedly missed just 27 minutes of the more than 1,700 minutes the Eskimos played in twenty-nine games over 117 days in 1926 and early 1927. At the beginning of the season he weighed 210 pounds. At the end of the road trip he was 185, dripping wet.

"Here's something that will tell you the type of fellow he was," Haugsrud said in *The Game That Was*. "The league had me put a clause into his contract saying that he had to be in each game a certain number of minutes. I think it was twenty-five minutes. But when Ernie read that clause he said, 'Ole, you can shove this up yours and up Joe Carr's, too!' It provoked him that the league thought he was the kind of guy who would want to be out of the game. I said to him, 'Ernie it'd just be a lot of trouble for me to go back to the league and get this clause out, so what's the difference?' We left it in, but Ernie took it as an insult to his integrity."

The 1926 Duluth Eskimos team "was the game's most durable and most responsive...I've seen in more than fifty years in sports," Haugsrud continued. "When they selected the charter members of the Pro Football Hall of Fame...three of the first seventeen men enshrined were on that Eskimos team: Nevers, Johnny Blood, and Walt Kiesling. That should give you some idea of the talent we had."

The manager was good, too, Haugsrud wrote: "Dewey Scanlon was a big asset to our ball club with his ability to substitute at the right time, changing position of players on defense and offense."

Of the tour, Haugsrud said, "It was a lot of work and a lot of exciting fun, too. No football team, amateur or pro, in world sports history, has ever accomplished a similar feat. And to add to the glory of this unique accomplishment we did it with a squad of thirteen players 75 percent of the time. Think that one over. Twenty-nine football battles in one season with thirteen performers."

And on top of that, Nevers had made history in 1926 by playing three different professional sports in the same year. He had pitched for the St. Louis Browns in the spring and summer, laced up his football boots in the fall for the Eskimos, and then, starting that winter, he put on his basketball shoes for the Chicago Bruins of the American Basketball League, the first true professional basketball association in the United States.

～

The on-the-road success of the Duluth Eskimos was a hot topic of conversation at the NFL's annual league meeting in February 1927. It had to be. There was little else positive to talk about in the league. The Roaring Twenties were roaring to a close, and fans were growing weary of the slow, plodding play of professional football. The excitement of Babe Ruth–style home run bashing had made baseball America's pastime.

Most of the NFL's teams were in deep financial trouble, and league President Joe Carr knew he had to take serious, dramatic, and immediate action to save his league. On April 23, he called a special meeting in Cleveland with one word on the agenda: reorganization. Under Carr's guidance, a difficult decision was made to eliminate its financially weaker franchises and to redistribute their best players to the more successful clubs.

The struggling teams were given a choice. They either could disband entirely, taking with them a pro-rated portion of the league's treasury, or they could disband for a year to sell their players and search for new, league-approved ownership, which could result in a bigger payday.

By the middle of July, twelve of the NFL's franchises opted to suspend operations for the year. They were the Akron Indians, Brooklyn Lions, Columbus Tigers, Detroit Panthers, Hammond Pros, Hartford Blues, Kansas City Cowboys, Los Angeles Buccaneers, Louisville Colonels, Milwaukee Badgers, Minneapolis Marines, and Rochester Jeffersons. Kansas City was the first of the group to then disband entirely. The Cowboys' owners sold or canceled all of their players' contracts. Their popular pregame horse parades became a thing of the past.

The ten teams that remained from 1926—including the reigning NFL-champion Frankford Yellow Jackets, Tim Mara's New York Giants, the Green Bay Packers, Chicago Bears, Providence Steam Roller, Pottsville Maroons, Chicago Cardinals, Dayton Triangles, Duluth Eskimos, and Buffalo Bisons (formerly the Rangers)—were joined for the 1927 season by the Cleveland Bulldogs, who returned after temporarily suspending operations a year earlier, and the New York Yankees.

The American Football League that Pyle and Grange created, the league that had threatened the very existence of the NFL just the year before, was now dead. The Yankees, its only team to enjoy even moderate success, was granted Brooklyn's NFL franchise, but with one condition. To appease Mara's territorial concerns, the Yankees agreed to play thirteen of their sixteen games on the road in 1927.

～

The Eskimos retained a strong nucleus of players from a 1926 team that finished with a .545 winning percentage—not counting the many exhibition games played from Portland, Maine, to San Francisco. Nevers returned for another year to handle the bulk of the running, passing, and kicking. Also back were the other hall-of-famers-to-be: two-way guard Walt Kiesling and vagabond halfback Johnny Blood McNally. Russ Method, one of Nevers' favorite passing targets, returned for a fifth season of pro ball in his hometown. Center Bill Stein also returned for his fifth year in Duluth. And the Rooney brothers were back, all three of them—Bill, Cobb, and Joe—on the same roster for the first time since 1924. Of an estimated three hundred sets of siblings to have played in the NFL, they're believed to have been the only set of three brothers to be on the same team at the same time. (All three also suited up for the 1929 Chicago Cardinals)

But the Eskimos also lost some key contributors from the previous season, of few of them, undoubtedly, because they were worn out from the grind of the road trip.

No loss was bigger than that of team manager Dewey Scanlon, who had been chosen by pro football's sportswriters as coach of the year in 1925, along with the Chicago Bears' George "Papa Bear" Halas and the Detroit Panthers' Jimmy Conzelman. Scanlon walked away from pro football with a record of seventeen wins, fifteen losses, and four ties.

Wally Gilbert ended the pro football portion of his illustrious athletic career after three memorable seasons with the Kelley-Duluth team and one with the Eskimos. He had been "one of Wrigley's best customers" Haugsrud once joked. "He would chew two packages of gum before each game." Paul Fitzgibbon, the "Red-Haired Flash," went to the Frankford Yellow Jackets in 1927, playing eleven games. Finally, after being long sought by Bears' management, he would wind up in Chicago. Lineman Oke Carlson, probably best remembered for his egg-munching stunt at training camp a year earlier, retired from football after eighteen games over three seasons in Duluth. And Doc Kelly similarly quit football after three years and thirteen games in Duluth.

Haugsrud was forced to retool his lineup the best he could. He plugged holes with rookies and with castoffs from belly-up franchises. From the defunct Milwaukee Badgers he signed Marion Charles "Bert" Ashmore, a six foot, 215-pound, twenty-eight-year-old end, guard, and tackle who grew up in Illinois and attended college at Gonzaga. Also from the Badgers came Clement Francis "Clem" Neacy, a six-foot-three, 206-pound lineman. He grew up in Milwaukee, attended South Division High School there, and played football for New York's Colgate University.

The rookies included another Illinois native, Charles William "Bunny" Belden of Chicago. The twenty-six-year-old fullback, halfback, and quarterback stood five feet eight inches tall and weighed 173 pounds. He attended Visalia High School and St. Mary's College, both in California. Alfred C. "Potts" or "Potsy" Clarke, was a twenty-six-year-old rookie halfback, quarterback, and tackle who stood five feet seven inches tall, weighed 180 pounds, and played college football for Nevada-Reno. James H. "Chick" or "Tex" Lang was another rookie. The twenty-six-year-old guard attended Harrison High School in Chicago. John Lacey "Jack" McCarthy was a 186-pound rookie tackle from California. William "Bill" McNellis was a five-foot-eleven, 177-pound rookie fullback and quarterback from Duluth Denfeld High School and St. Mary's College in Winona, Minnesota. Other new Eskimos included an end and guard named Lawrence "Fritz" Cronin and a 214-pound tackle and halfback named Shanley.

He had a seventeen-player roster, a full team by Eskimos standards, but Haugsrud wasn't able to schedule games the first three weeks of the season, nor the fifth week.

"We couldn't get the games we needed," he complained in *The Game That Was*. "One reason was the league cut down from twenty-two clubs to twelve and another reason was that we were asking a $4,000 guarantee and the weaker clubs would rather schedule a team that asked, say, $1,500 less."

Haugsrud offered another explanation to football historian Ralph Hickok: "With the AFL threat ended and Grange now playing for his own team, the New York Yankees, in the NFL, owners weren't so eager to schedule the Eskimos, and fans weren't so eager to see Nevers," he said.

It was a slow and ominous start to the new season.

NINE

GONE, NOT FORGOTTEN

Duluth finally opened its 1927 season on October 9 against Curly Lambeau and the Packers in Green Bay. The weather was dry and crisp, a perfect autumn afternoon. Some five thousand fans, including a small delegation from Duluth, filled Green Bay's City Stadium with an electric buzz.

The tension built through a scoreless first quarter. In the second quarter, a long pass from Lambeau to Verne Lewellen put the ball near the Eskimos' goal line. From there, Lewellen, a former collegiate star for the University of Nebraska, plunged over for the touchdown. Four-year pro Red Dunn added the extra point, booting a placed ball through the uprights. At the end of the half it was the Packers in the lead, 7-0.

In the third quarter Nevers hit Blood McNally for thirty-five yards through the air. He wasn't pulled down until he reached the Packers' fifteen-yard line. The Eskimos looked to tie the game, but then rookie Potsy Clarke lost five yards on a line plunge, and Nevers had a pass knocked down by Lavern "Lavvie" Dilweg, the Packers second-year left end. Attempting to pass again on the next play, Nevers instead was chased backward and dumped for a twenty-yard loss. His next pass was knocked down, allowing Green Bay to take possession and punt out of danger.

The Packers scored two more times in the fourth quarter, the final touchdown from Dilweg, a Milwaukee Marquette University standout who picked off a pass by Nevers and raced twenty yards into the Eskimos' end zone, yielding a 20-0 shutout. The Eskimos pulled out of Wisconsin, heading east on another lengthy road trip to Pottsville, Pennsylvania, home of the Pottsville Maroons, who were coming off an outstanding ten-win, two-loss, and one-tie season.

The Eskimos were able to start hot and stay hot the chilly afternoon of October 23, 1927. Duluth connected on twenty-six passes, Joe Rooney scored three touchdowns, Russ Method added another, and Ernie Nevers converted three extra points.

The Eskimos won convincingly, shutting out the mighty Maroons, 27-0, to even their record at one win and one loss. "The Pottsville fans gave the Eskimos a rousing reception at the close of the game, although the local eleven has not suffered such a lopsided defeat in several years," the Associated Press reported. The win came at a steep price, however. Potsy Clarke, "the dashing little halfback," as the Associated Press called him, was carried off the field with a broken collar bone.

~

The following week, on the day before Halloween, Nevers played one of his greatest games in an Eskimos uniform. He proved why he was so often referred to as a one-man team. He scored all twenty of Duluth's points against the Benny Friedman-led Cleveland Bulldogs. But it turned out not to be enough. In a heart-breaker, the Eskimos fell 21-20.

Duluth played well again the following week, on November 6, in a game against the New York Giants at the Polo Grounds. A gigantic crowd of some twenty thousand filled the seats and watched as the Eskimos racked up eighteen first downs to the Giants' eleven and completed eighteen passes to the Giants' twelve. Duluth marched six times inside New York's twenty-yard line. Those stats looked good, but, despite "clearly outplaying the Giants...the Eskimos lacked the final 'punch' to score in the game today," the Associated Press reported.

Meanwhile, the Giants marched forty yards on a drive early in the game and handed the ball to Mule Wilson, a five-foot-eleven, 192-pound fireplug of a back who had played college ball for Texas A&M. Mule punched it in to give his team the lead. Doug Wycoff, a product of Georgia Tech, used his six-foot frame to intercept an Eskimos' pass. He lumbered his 206-pound girth into the end zone for another Giants' score. Hinkey Haines, the former Penn State quarterback, scampered thirty-five yards around end for a third New York touchdown. And Jack McBride of Syracuse added three extra-point kicks to give the home team a 21-0 shutout.

After playing an exhibition game in Wilkes-Barre, Pennsylvania, the Eskimos continued their league schedule on November 13 against the Steam Roller at the Providence Cycledrome in Rhode Island.

Desperate for a return to the win column, Duluth started fast once again with Nevers scoring a touchdown in the opening quarter on a thirty-six-yard scamper through the defensive line. He added the extra-point and, just four minutes into the game, the Eskimos led 7-0.

Providence evened the score soon enough, however. Its standout end Jack Spellman scooped up a loose ball at midfield that had been fumbled by Blood McNally. Spellman raced to the Duluth nine-yard line. Bill Cronin took the ball from there, sprinting into the end zone. Gus Sonnenberg added the extra point.

Similar to the game against the Giants, the Eskimos drove the ball deep into the Providence territory time after time, six times in all. But, also like in the Giants game, Duluth was "checked by the local team or lost the ball on fumbles or penalties," according to the Associated Press report. "The Duluth gridders lacked the necessary punch to score."

The assessment was beginning to sound familiar.

Providence won the game late in the fourth quarter on Curley Oden's "brilliant" seventy-four-yard punt return for a touchdown. The Eskimos lost again, this time by a score of 13-7.

Following yet another exhibition game, this one in Springfield, Massachusetts, the Eskimos lined up on Sunday, November 20, in Pottsville, Pennsylvania, the site of their 27-0 victory a month earlier. This time, however, the Eskimos ended up on the short end of a 6-0 shutout.

Six days after that, Nevers' team failed to score once again and lost 6-0 to the Frankford Yellow Jackets. Duluth's win-loss record dropped to a dismal 1-6. And then to an even more dismal 1-7 on December 3, when the road-weary Eskimos were shut out for a third straight week, 20-0, to the Cleveland Bulldogs.

Duluth's final game of the year brought them closer to home. On December 11, they lined up against the Chicago Bears, one of three teams still in contention for the league championship. Duluth was eager to finish the season on an up note, but the Bears drew first blood. Three long passes by Paddy Driscoll, the last one into the end zone to fifth-year veteran Laurie Walquist of Rockford, Illinois, gave Chicago the early lead.

Duluth, showing no quit, scored twice in the second quarter to snatch back the lead. Both touchdowns came through the air, the first from Nevers to Blood McNally and the second from Nevers to Cobb Rooney. Duluth took a 14-6 lead into halftime.

But that was when "the Bears buckled down to business," as the Associated Press reported. Chicago regained the lead in the third quarter on a forty-five-yard touchdown run around end by Driscoll.

With time running down, Nevers tried to pass his Eskimos back into the lead. But the Bears picked off one of his heaves and returned the ball forty yards for a third touchdown. They added a final score late in the game on a pass to Driscoll by twenty-seven-year-old Joey Sternaman. Remember him? He had been the quarterback and leader of the Kelley-Duluth team in 1923.

The "Chicago Bears Rally to Score 27-to-14 Victory Over Eskimos," the middle-of-the-sports-page headline read the following morning in the *Duluth News Tribune*. Banner headlines for the Eskimos had weeks earlier become a thing of the past back home.

With a record of one win and eight losses, the Eskimos finished eleventh in the NFL in 1927—second to last. The Buffalo Bisons were twelfth, with five losses and no wins.

"We found the going tougher.... Our players were getting older and couldn't be expected to go through such another grueling season as the previous one," Haugsrud wrote of his Eskimos' 1927 season. "We did not win as many games, but we came through all right financially."

All right financially—but definitely not "all right" enough. "We [had] made a profit of a few thousand in 1926," Haugsrud said in *The Game That Was*. "But [in 1927] we came out only about a thousand ahead."

~

By the time the Eskimos struggled through their last game of the season, the NFL championship was already decided. In late November only three of the twelve teams had still been in the hunt. The New York Giants—at eight wins, one loss, and one tie—held a slim lead in the standings. The Chicago Bears had seven wins, one loss, and one tie, and the Green Bay Packers had six wins, one loss, and one tie.

On November 20, the Bears had beat the Packers, 14-6, to set up a championship showdown the following Sunday between the Bears and Giants. That Thursday, in a Thanksgiving Day matchup, the Bears slipped, losing to their crosstown rivals, the Chicago Cardinals, 3-0. The win was one of only three the Cardinals would have all season. On Sunday, in the game to crown the champion, the Bears lost to the Giants, 13-7. New York's hall-of-fame tackle Steve Owen called the showdown "the toughest, roughest football game I ever played." Adding in their exhibition games, the NFL-champion Giants had recorded ten shutouts in their eleven wins for the 1927 season. Their only loss and only tie had both been against the Cleveland Bulldogs; the Bulldogs finished the season in fourth place with eight wins, four losses, and one tie. Grange's New York Yankees had wrapped up their first NFL season in sixth place and in financial trouble. Just four weeks into the 1927 campaign, in a game against the Chicago Bears, Grange went down with a crippling knee injury. Although he missed only three weeks of action, he "was just an ordinary ball carrier after that," as he himself later admitted. Although he "did develop into a pretty good defensive back," the crowds stopped coming out to see him play.

~

In the spring of 1928, Nevers started pitching his final season for the Browns, helping St. Louis to a terrific 82-72 win-loss record and a third-place league finish. Nearly 340,000 fans turned out for Browns' home games that year at Sportsman's Park III.

Nevers' brief baseball career, hampered by injuries no doubt related to the beatings he took on the football field, had lasted just three seasons. He played in forty-five games and had sixty at bats, scoring twice and recording twelve runs and a run batted in. He struck out eighteen times en route to a career batting average of .200. Not that he didn't start out hot at the plate. In his very first at bat, against the Washington Senators' great Walter Johnson, Nevers had knocked a double, his only one of the 1926 season and one of only two in his career.

As a pitcher, he struck out thirty-nine batters, walked sixty-one, and won six games while losing twelve and saving two others. He tallied 178.1 innings in forty-four games, giving up 196 hits and ninety-two earned runs for an earned run average, or ERA, of 4.64. Nevers had served up thirteen home run balls, two of them to Babe Ruth during his record-setting sixty-home-run season of 1927. Ruth hit Nos. 8 and 41 off Nevers.

"I don't feel too badly though," Nevers once commented, according to the Pro Football Hall of Fame. "[The Babe] hit a lot of pitchers—some them good, too." Ruth had nothing but praise for Nevers' best pitch, his fastball. "You've got good speed, kid," Ruth said. "For my sake, I hope you stick to football."

~

With the baseball season over, Nevers—instead of returning to the gridiron with Duluth, where he had compiled 102 points in two memorable seasons—headed west to coach for Glenn "Pop" Warner at his alma mater Stanford. Coaching would be physically easier on Nevers, who needed a break from the demands and injuries of pro football.

Without Nevers, Haugsrud knew his prospects for profits were slim at best in 1928. Unable to field a competitive team, the proud Swede made the hard decision to suspend operations for the year. His players found other places to scrimmage. Walt Kiesling and Blood McNally both ended up with the Pottsville Maroons for the 1928 season. The following season Nevers returned to playing football with the Chicago Cardinals. He rejoined former Duluth teammates Kiesling, Chick Lang, Mickey McDonnell, Russ Method, Bill and Cobb Rooney, Bill Stein, and Jack Underwood; McNally moved to the Packers.

Haugsrud was far from alone in his troubles. The NFL had continued its push for fewer, more profitable teams rather than the abundance of struggling franchises that had marked the league's tenuous existence. The owners of the Cleveland Bulldogs, despite a successful eight-win, four-loss and one-tie record in 1927, also suspended operations. So did the Buffalo Bisons, who hadn't won a game in two years.

Franchises that had suspended operations before the 1927 season but hadn't sold were permanently canceled by the league on July 7. Those teams were the Akron Indians, Columbus Tigers, Hammond Pros, Hartford Blues, Los Angeles Buccaneers, Louisville Colonels, Milwaukee Badgers, Minneapolis Marines, and Rochester Jeffersons. With the Detroit Wolverines the only added franchise, the league faced the 1928 season with just ten organizations.

The Providence Steam Roller, led by Jimmy Conzelman and Pearce Johnson, won the league championship in 1928, winning eight times against only one loss and two ties. Their Cycledrome rocked with enthusiasm during every Providence home game.

~

The league, lean but financially stronger than it ever had been, would weather the Great Depression and grow steadily. But only one small-town franchise survived the Great Depression and exists today: the publicly owned Green Bay

Packers. Could Duluth have been another Green Bay? *Duluth News Tribune* sportswriter Bruce Bennett put the question to Haugsrud in 1975. Haugsrud responded:

> Who's to say? Who knew back in the Twenties that football would blossom thirty years later? But the ingredients were there. I suppose if I had been a little older and knew a little more, had a little more experience, I'd have had the guts to go to the mining people and say, 'Look, here's an opportunity to do something.' Then maybe we could have stayed in the league.
>
> I think the one big comparison between Duluth and Green Bay was that they had a good, young, energetic group and Curly Lambeau was the fellow who got them going. It was about that time that the paper mills were coming into Green Bay and there are…big mills down there now.
>
> Those…mills were naturally looking for young people. You think of New York and Chicago as big cities, and they were in those days, but jobs were tough to get. In Green Bay they had jobs to offer, and good ones.
>
> And when the Packers started winning and winning championships, [the paper firms] would send these young men all over the country introducing their products. They'd tell them they were from Green Bay and the people would say, "Oh, you know about the Green Bay Packers?" It was an easy foot in the door.

Could the mining companies of Northeastern Minnesota have supported the Eskimos the way the paper companies of Northeastern Wisconsin helped the Packers? Maybe. A shame they were never asked. Today, professional football is a Sunday-afternoon (and Sunday night, Monday night, and some Thursday nights) American institution as well as a multi-billion-dollar industry.

~

In 1929, the same year Wall Street crashed, sending the U.S. into the tailspin of the Great Depression, Haugsrud was forced to sell his dormant and financially challenged team. He was able to hammer out a deal at the league meetings, held that year in Cleveland. He insisted on $3,000 for the Eskimos, but an investment group from Orange, New Jersey (the Orange Athletic Club wanted to take its independent team pro) was refusing to budge from its $2,000 offer. Meanwhile, as the negotiations continued, other team owners were growing antsy. They didn't want to have to pony up for another night in the high-priced hotel that hosted the NFL's annual gathering. Their lack of patience benefited the shrewd Haugsrud.

"Come on, Swede," the owners begged. "We've got to get going home."

"All right," Haugsrud finally relented, taking the $2,000, "but with one stipulation: The next time a franchise is granted in the state of Minnesota, I will have the first opportunity to bid for it."

The owners agreed, drafting a letter that Haugsrud would never let them forget. Neither would his long-time friend, the Chicago Bears' George "Papa Bear" Halas. The arrangement wouldn't bear fruit for more than three decades—a long time to hold on to a promissory note, but hold on to it Haugsrud did.

~

The Duluth Eskimos didn't just fade into the annals of NFL history. The franchise, as the Orange Tornadoes in New Jersey, played an average season in 1929, winning three games, losing four, and tying four to finish sixth in a twelve-team league dominated by the champion Green Bay Packers.

In 1930 the franchise moved to larger Newark, New Jersey, becoming the Newark Tornadoes. A miserable season followed. The Tornadoes won only once while losing ten games and tying one time to finish dead last in what had become an eleven-team league. The Packers again won the championship.

Before 1931, the franchise, struggling right along with the American economy, was forfeited to the league. The NFL, in an unprecedented move, ordered that the team be sold to the highest bidder before the new season began. But no bids were received before play started, and without the Tornadoes, the NFL shrank to ten teams. Then, halfway through the year, the once-proud Frankford Yellow Jackets also folded. And, in a sign of just how disorganized and precarious the league and its teams were becoming, the Green Bay Packers, Portsmouth Spartans, and Chicago Bears were each fined $1,000 by the league for illegally using college players.

Despite the penalties, the three teams finished first, second, and third in 1931, the Packers' third straight league title. The Wisconsinites finished a game better than the Spartans, who were led by rookie backs Earl "Dutch" Clark and Glenn Presnell.

With the Depression draining the nation's spirit right along with its bank accounts, NFL membership in 1932 fell to an all-time low of just eight teams.

The Cleveland Indians disappeared. And the Providence Steam Roller, just four years removed from an NFL championship, suspended operations with league permission. The team never reorganized.

One new team emerged in 1932, however. In July, investors from Boston—including George Preston Marshall, Vincent Bendix, Jay O'Brien, and M. Dorland Doyle—were granted a franchise. They were given the forfeited Newark Tornadoes franchise, according to Haugsrud and others—the franchise that had once been the Eskimos and that had been available to the highest bidder. In interviews and in letters Haugsrud wrote in 1962 to the *Green Bay Press Gazette* and in 1974 to the Chicago Bears' George "Papa Bear" Halas, Haugsrud claimed that the investment group led by Marshall was that "highest bidder," even if its bid had come in long after the start of the 1931 season.

The Marshall group's timing couldn't have been worse. Millions of Americans were out of work, many of them standing in soup lines and without the disposable income needed to attend football games. Before the season was over, the Marshall team—the Boston Braves, as they were called because they played at Braves Field, the major league baseball team's home park—was in the hole $46,000. It also was down three owners, with Marshall the only one of the original investors to stick it out. He undoubtedly was encouraged by the future hall-of-famers he had on his roster, namely halfback Cliff Battles and tackle Glen "Turk" Edwards, both rookies. Battles led the NFL in rushing in 1932 with 576 yards, a 3.9 yards-per-carry average and three touchdowns. The league kept official statistics for the first time that year.

Hoping to reverse his team's financial fortunes, Marshall moved to Boston's famous Fenway Park in 1933, changing the team's name to the Redskins. It didn't make much difference. The money-losing, 4-4 Boston Braves of 1932 became the money-losing, 5-5 Boston Redskins of 1933.

Attendance and fan support became such a problem in Bean Town that when the Redskins won the Eastern Division championship in 1936 and qualified to host the league championship game, Marshall moved the matchup out of Fenway Park and into New York's Polo Grounds. Without home-field support, his team lost 21-6 to the team from Titletown, USA, the Green Bay Packers.

On February 13, 1937, Marshall moved the Redskins to their modern-day home of Washington, D.C. In the nation's capital, the team finally flourished. The Redskins signed All-American tailback Sammy Baugh of Texas Christian University, and, playing in Griffith Stadium, they won the 1937 league championship 28-21 over the Chicago Bears. Marshall—"a master showman" who "brought a ton of popularity to pro football," as Haugsrud once said of him—created an official marching band for his team and a fight song for his fans. Both were firsts for the NFL. Under his leadership, the Redskins proved to be a groundbreaking NFL team. A lot like the Duluth Eskimos before them.

"Much credit should be given Marshall for the way he handled the former Duluth franchise and developed it to the point it is today in Washington," Haugsrud said. "He is a most likable fellow."

~

In a league where official statistics weren't even recorded prior to 1932, however—five years after the Eskimos played their final game—not everyone believes that the Washington Redskins are the same franchise that was started by Kelley Hardware in Duluth. Jon Winter of Superior, Wisconsin, has researched the story and called the oft-repeated lineage an "urban legend." In the *Duluth News Tribune* in December 2006, Winter said:

> I've been after this for almost 25 years. [Ever since] I was in ninth-grade doing a report for English class, and I figured, "Something isn't right." I could never find any documentation, nothing other than what's written in books [or repeated in magazine or newspaper articles]. I could never find an historical NFL reference, minutes from a league meeting or anything. Every other time a franchise moved and was renamed, there was documentation, it seemed. I couldn't find any documentation. I couldn't find any proof.

Winter did find one document that suggested the Marshall group had been granted "the inactive Boston franchise," not the former Newark Tornadoes, as Haugsrud always claimed. The "inactive Boston franchise" would have been the Boston Bulldogs, which operated for one year in 1929, and which was the former Pottsville, Pennsylvania, Maroons.

Official histories of the Redskins—according to the team and the Professional Football Hall of Fame—state the franchise started in 1932 as the Boston Braves. Neither written history dates to the Kelley-Duluth team or to the Duluth Eskimos. Of course, the Redskins don't acknowledge the Boston Bulldogs connection, either, according to Winter, who interviewed team historians in 2002. Duluth's official pro-football history, according to the Hall of Fame, ends in 1929 in Orange, New Jersey.

"I don't think there's a genuinely definitive answer," wrote Ralph Hickok, who penned an article for *Sports Illustrated* about the barnstorming 1926 Eskimos. "I discovered that there simply wasn't much reliable sports reference material out there. Sports history, insofar as it existed at all, was largely a morass of myth and legend, misinformation, misspelled names, and misplaced dates."

Ross Bernstein faced similar difficulties while researching *Pigskin Pride*, his 2002 book about the history of Minnesota football. "Those teams were all vagabond teams back then," he said. "When teams were bought and sold, everything was bought and sold, the uniforms, the balls, everything…. I believe the lineage that starts with the Kelleys ends with the Redskins. Anyone who could dispute that is long dead. I'll go to my grave saying that and believing that."

The debate is a lively one, and Winter is content with leaving it that way. That is the same way he ended his ninth-grade English report. His teacher gave him an A-plus. The Eskimos-to-Redskins evolution "could be proved, there is a possibility," Winter admitted, even if the only proof seems to be "just what everyone says."

Of course, that "everyone" includes Haugsrud. Who was there. Who knew as well as anybody.

TEN

"UNCLE OLE" RETURNS

After his beloved Eskimos were sold and gone, Ole Haugsrud drifted to Chicago and worked as the Cardinals' business manager. He then practiced public relations for the Detroit Lions and scouted for the New York Giants.

Returning to Duluth in 1933, Haugsrud had a new business venture in mind, one outside of football—but not completely out of sports.

A year earlier, a desperate America had elected Franklin Delano Roosevelt as president, hoping he could pull the nation out of the economic chaos and rampant unemployment of the Great Depression. Roosevelt's "New Deal" strategy for recovery included the $3 billion Civilian Conservation Corps. With 4,500 camps all over the U.S., including some in northern Minnesota, the corps gave jobs and purpose to more than three million men over nine years. The Corps built 125,000 miles of roads, strung 89,000 miles of phone lines, and constructed 13,100 miles of foot trails. Workers stocked 972 million fish, restored 3,980 historic structures, planted more than two billion trees, and constructed eight hundred state parks and fifty-two thousand acres of public campgrounds. Their erosion control programs benefited 40 million farm acres; their shoreline protection work saved 154 million square yards of riverbanks and lake edges.

In 1933, when the camps were first opening, Haugsrud launched CCC Canteen Service, a series of stores that served the camps and that were staffed by previously out-of-work football players and other athletes. His idea proved successful even after 1942, when the CCC camps closed, and Haugsrud opened his "canteen service" in Duluth. He sold candy, tobacco, and other convenience items. In 1965, he sold the business to Twin Ports Wholesale Grocers.

~

Although he was no longer an NFL team owner, Haugsrud continued to faith-
fully attend the annual league meetings. His friendship with New York Giants
coach Steve Owen led to that team, during the 1940s, conducting preseason
training camps at the campus of the Superior State Teacher's College, now the
University of Wisconsin-Superior. Haugsrud, his connections and his other
business ventures—including Minnesota Sports, Inc. and Tri-State Sports
Enterprises—also brought the Chicago Cardinals to the Twin Ports for training camps and the Philadelphia Eagles and Green Bay Packers for practices in
Grand Rapids, Minnesota, about eighty-five miles west of Duluth.

Finally, in 1960, Haugsrud's decades-old letter from NFL owners paid off.

The growing Twin Cities area was among the largest metropolitan regions in the United States without professional football or baseball. Hoping
to change that, the city of Minneapolis built Metropolitan Stadium on the site
of what is today the Mall of America.

The former owner of the Minneapolis Lakers professional basketball team,
Max Winter, then went to work putting together a group to bring pro football
back to the Gopher State. Winter's group—which also included Minneapolis
businessmen Bill Boyer and H. P. Skoglund—negotiated with both the NFL
and the upstart American Football League, hoping to sweeten a deal by pitting
the two rival leagues against one another.

The AFL seemed to have won out when the men put down a deposit on
a yet-unnamed AFL franchise and even participated in the AFL's first player draft. Winter's group picked University of Wisconsin quarterback Dale
Hackbart (who would later play defensive back for the Vikings). But that's
when the NFL called to say it had a franchise waiting for Minnesota.

Winter and his partners abandoned the AFL in favor of the long-estab-
lished NFL. The newcomer league objected, of course, and even threatened to
sue. The AFL calmed down, however, when it was able to transfer the Minneapolis franchise to Oakland where it would become the Oakland Raiders.

Joining the NFL required more money than Winter, Boyer, and Skoglund
had been prepared to invest in entering the AFL. So millionaire Bernard Ridder, *St. Paul Dispatch and Pioneer Press* publisher, stepped in and bought 30
percent ownership of the team.

The return of the NFL to Minnesota also brought into play Haugsrud's
decades-old agreement. Invited to plunk down $60,000 to purchase a 10 per-

cent share of the Vikings. Haugsrud happily did so. Some say he also named the team, perhaps in honor of his Superior Central High School Vikings, whose uniforms were purple and white.

In the November 1986 issue of *Mpls. St. Paul Magazine*, Kevin Reichard wrote:

> It was an odd arrangement. Winter was a hustler from north Minne-apolis, a man who had spent the better part of his life promoting pro basketball, auto shows, and movie theaters. Boyer was a Minnesota car dealer who had somehow acquired an authentic-sounding Southern drawl. Ridder seemed more at home at the country club than on the sidelines. Skoglund was a self-made millionaire through his insurance company and was a friend of Scandinavian royalty. And Haugsrud—well, Haugsrud was what you'd expect of a football promoter from the 1930s: cigar wedged into the side of his mouth, ever ready to tell a tale of what the old days were like.

An owner once again in the NFL, Haugsrud enjoyed renewed fame back home in the Twin Ports. Accolades poured in. In 1962, he was named the thirty-eighth member of the Duluth Hall of Fame, an honor given annually to the city's most outstanding citizen. "This recognition is probably the highest honor I'll receive in my lifetime," a typically gracious Haugsrud said at the time.

In 1963, Duluth's Noon Optimist Club named Haugsrud its Optimist of the Year "for outstanding endeavors on behalf of Duluth and for his many contributions and his interest and help for the youth of Duluth."

Haugsrud more than fit the billing. He was active with the Duluth Fatherless Boys Association, providing candy for parties and his boat for outings. He was well known for taking Duluth children—lots of them—to the Twin Cities for Minnesota Vikings games. He paid tuitions, or goodly portions of tuitions, that allowed numerous Duluth youth to go to college who otherwise wouldn't have had the opportunity. And he bought the first football uniforms for the team at Father Flanagan's Boys' Home in Omaha, Nebraska. (Now Girls and Boys Town, the organization treats and cares for abused, abandoned, and neglected children.) Haugsrud had first met Flanagan during high school while traveling with his Red Devils basketball team. He recalled:

> There was this…bunch of little boys. They all had musical instruments and looked like they were some sort of boys' band. [Father Flanagan]

struck up a conversation with me and told me about a boys' town he was starting in Nebraska and was going around with the band trying to raise money.... When we got off the train at the next town, I gave him a basketball and we became very good friends. Years later, when he was starting a football team after boys' town had become a reality, he asked me for help again, and I was able to secure some discarded uniforms of the New York Giants for him. I'll never forget what he said when I told him the uniforms might be a little large for high school boys: "Ole, one thing we've got a lot of here is seamstresses."

In 1965, Haugsrud received the Viking Ring, presented annually for life-time contributions to Minnesota sports. Minneapolis sportswriter Dick Cullum presented the ring to Haugsrud, saying: "Despite losing his franchise, Ole didn't miss a league meeting since 1922 and was a driving force behind Minnesota's obtaining a franchise in 1960.... Ole was the only man determined that we would have professional football return to Minnesota some day. When the Vikings franchise was awarded his job was fulfilled." The 1,500 Minnesotans in attendance at the ceremony in Minneapolis gave Haugsrud a well-deserved standing ovation.

In 1966, when Duluth's new $6.2 million arena opened on the Duluth-Superior Harbor, Haugsrud helped to arrange its first attraction: a basketball clinic for kids and an exhibition game between the Los Angeles Lakers and the Cincinnati Royals. Haugsrud and his Tri-State Enterprises also donated the backboard mechanisms to the new arena at a cost of nearly $5,000. The hydraulic jack–operated collapsible structures could raise the hoops to the regulation ten feet and then lower them into their own frames for compact storage. The frames, coated in thick foam rubber for safety, were used by the Duluth Entertainment Convention Center until 2004.

In 1968, Haugsrud was one of three members of the inaugural class of the Duluth Arena Sports Hall of Fame. The hall honors Duluth-area athletes and sportsmen who gain national prominence. Haugsrud was joined by football great Bronislau "Bronko" Nagurski and boxer Billy "Fargo Express" Petrolle. Nagurski had helped the University of Minnesota Gophers to a Big Ten championship in 1927 and was an All-American on both sides of the ball, as a tackle and a fullback. His legend grew with the Chicago Bears from 1930 to 1937; after a five year retirement (which included a detour into professional wrestling) he returned to the Bears in 1943 for a final season. He had been enshrined as a charter member of the Pro Football Hall of Fame in 1963. He died in January 1990 at the age of eighty-one, after many years operating a gas station in International Falls, Minnesota, where he grew up. Petrolle had turned pro boxer in 1922 at the tender age of seventeen. He retired in 1934 after 160 official fights (but perhaps after as many as 250 or more bouts), including 10 matches against current or past world champions. He won half of those. Petrolle ran a religious-goods business in Duluth for more than twenty years and was also a bank director. He died in 1983 in Vero Beach, Florida. Inducted posthumously in the International Boxing Hall of Fame of Canastota, New York, in 2000, the crowd at Madison Square Garden reportedly gave him a standing ovation.

~

In 1969, Haugsrud, then the secretary of the board of directors for the Minnesota Vikings as well as an owner, was inducted into the Superior Athletic Hall of Fame. Five years before, the hall's inaugural class had included Haugsrud's Superior Central classmate Ernie Nevers as well as National League shortstop and big-league manager Dave Bancroft, the player whose bat Haugsrud had carried as a boy at Superior's Hislop Park.

"It embarrasses me," Haugsrud said at the induction ceremony, which was held in the Rothwell Student Center on the campus of what then was called Superior State. "There are so many great athletes, and I wasn't an athlete. I just happened to manage good teams that met with success."

Sportscaster Ray Scott, best known for his broadcasts of Green Bay Packers football, was the ceremony's guest speaker. Haugsrud was one of four inductees, the others being New York Giants fullback Alphonse "Tuffy" Leemans, professional women's figure skating great Bess Erhardt—and Minnesota Vikings Head Coach Harry "Bud" Grant.

Grant had been born in Superior and graduated high school there in 1945. He was a two-time All-Big Ten end in football for the University of Minnesota Gophers, a two-year baseball star, and a three-year basketball regular. Drafted to play football by the Philadelphia Eagles in the first round of 1950, Grant chose instead to play basketball for the Minneapolis Lakers. He joined the Eagles in 1952 at the defensive end position. He switched to offense in 1953 and caught 56 passes for 997 yards and seven touchdowns.

Grant then signed to play for the Winnipeg Blue Bombers, leading the Canadian Football League in receptions three times over the next four seasons. He was named the Blue Bombers' coach in 1957, guiding the team to four Grey Cup championships. In ten years he piled up 102 victories against only 56 defeats and 2 ties.

The impressive win-loss record—and a visit in Winnipeg from Haugsrud, an old acquaintance from Superior—helped Grant become the Minnesota Vikings' head coach in 1967. A year later, "he launched the Vikings on a string of championship seasons rarely equaled in sports competition," according to the Pro Football Hall of Fame, which inducted Grant as a member in 1994. His Vikings won the Central Division championship ten times in eleven seasons, missing only in 1972. Another NFC Central title in 1980 gave Grant a total of eleven championship teams. He took the Vikings to the Super Bowl four times, an accomplishment in itself, although tarnished a bit by never taking home the trophy.

Grant retired permanently in 1985 after eighteen NFL seasons and a record of 168 wins, 108 losses, and 5 ties.

~

On March 13, 1976, following a brief illness, Ole Haugsrud died in Duluth at the age of seventy-three. In his last years, the man who had become known as "Mr. Football" and "Uncle Ole" in the Twin Ports and elsewhere had continued to use sports to reach out. The National Conference of Christians and Jews had honored Haugsrud with its 1973 Brotherhood of Man Through Sports award.

"He meant a whole lot to the league, particularly when the league was just getting started," Pittsburgh Steelers owner Art Rooney said. "I don't know that anyone was more interested in the league than Ole. His passing is a real loss. He was a great person."

Bud Grant said:

> Ole goes back a long ways; he was literally a friend of the family. My first contact with him was through my father. They were good friends when I was a boy. I think it is kind of ironic that I ended up working for Ole [as Vikings head coach]. My dad always thought a great deal of him and what an honorable man he was.
>
> He liked to stay in the background. It was only recently that you could get him to go to a dinner or anything and take a bow. He preferred a table in back. He was just a tremendous man and good friend.

Vikings President Max Winter said, "Certainly we'll miss Ole as a person, but [we] will also miss his counsel. There's no question…his death was a blow to the Minnesota Vikings, to all of us." Bernard Ridder, fellow Vikings owner and team board member, said:

> He was a grand gentleman and one of the real pioneers of professional football. Ole was the kind of man who still felt that professional football was first a sport and second a business. He believed in the best traditions of the sport and the world of professional football owes him a great debt for all the pioneering that he did. It was pioneers like George Halas, Art Rooney, George Preston Marshall, and Ole Haugsrud that made the game what it is today.

Bruce Bennett, longtime *Duluth News Tribune* sportswriter, authored Haugsrud's obituary: "Small in physical stature but big in heart and energy when it came to people and athletics, Ole Haugsrud will be missed by many. His influence extended seemingly everywhere in sport. Duluth, Superior, the region, and football have lost a wonderful friend and a genuine man."

Haugsrud's funeral was held in the church of his boyhood, Concordia Lutheran in Superior. Former Eskimos players were among the hundreds who attended. They included Doc Williams, Johnny Blood McNally, Joe Rooney, Jimmy Manion, Bill Stein, and Ernie Nevers, who was living then in California. Minnesota Vikings quarterback Fran Tarkenton called the former Margaret Peterman of Cloquet, Minnesota, Haugsrud's wife of nearly four decades, to offer his condolences.

The following September, Memorial Field, the football field at the University of Wisconsin-Superior, became the Ole Haugsrud Memorial Field after the university's chancellor Karl W. Meyer asked the University of Wisconsin System Board of Regents to approve the change.

~

A year and a half after her husband's death, Margaret Haugsrud agreed to sell Ole Haugsrud's 10 percent share of the Minnesota Vikings. "It was the right time to sell," she said in September 1977, while expressing an interest in maintaining some sort of tie to the team. She sold to three buyers: Vikings President Max Winter, the chairman of the Vikings board and team treasurer H. P. Skoglund, and board member Jack Steele. Winter and Skoglund had previously purchased Bernie Ridder's 30 percent interest in the team.

Haugsrud's ownership in the Vikings accounted for much of the $500,000-plus estate he left after his death. His decisions about how that money should be divided spoke volumes about what he considered important in life.

He left $1,000 to $5,000 to forty-five friends, relatives, and associates. His former business partner, Carl Olson, received $10,000. He gave $5,000 to Concordia Lutheran in memory of his parents; $1,000 each to surviving members of the Duluth Eskimos or their widows; $5,000 to Duluth Cathedral High School; and $1,000 each to the Duluth YMCA's Fatherless Boys Club, the Duluth Heart Fund, the Duluth Chapter of the American Cancer Society, and the Duluth Boys Club. Ernie Nevers' widow, Marjorie Nevers (Nevers died just a few months after Haugsrud's passing), received $5,000.

The balance of the estate went into two trusts, with the interest from both used to support his widow, who also received Rosemar, the couple's apartment and business building at 18 North Second Avenue East in downtown Duluth. After her death, one of the trusts was to be given 50 percent to the University of Minnesota Duluth Medical School, 25 percent to the University of Wisconsin-Superior, and the other 25 percent, in varying amounts, to Bemidji State University, St. Olaf College, the University of Minnesota, and Gustavus Adolphus College. The schools were required to use the bequests to assist deserving students, especially athletes, Ole Haugsrud stipulated.

"He was very kind and very generous," said Betty Bzoskie of Duluth, one of Haugsrud's cousins (her father and his father had emigrated from Norway together). "Both of them, him and Margaret, they were good people. They were very good people. One was as generous as the other. They had no children of their own, but they took care of an awful lot of kids."

Those kids included Bzoskie's daughter, who was able to attend the University of Minnesota in Minneapolis with tuition assistance from the Haugsruds. She studied physical therapy and became a physical therapist in Ada, Minnesota. Bzoskie said she and Margaret Haugsrud traveled often with the Vikings. She even had season tickets.

"[Ole] just gave us our tickets," she said. "We went to the Super Bowl in California and the one in New Orleans. That was the best of all. I think I'm a very, very lucky lady [to have been his cousin]. He was an important person. And he made a big difference in a lot of lives."

Few, if any, benefited more from the generosity of the Haugsruds than their eight nieces and nephews, who lived in Duluth and nearby Cloquet. The

Duluth relations hosted Easter every year, the family in Cloquet had everyone over for Christmas, and the Haugsruds, at their apartment in downtown
Duluth, put on the feast for Thanksgiving. Always with football on the TV.

"We were always watching," said Mary Peterman of Duluth, one of the
Haugsruds' nieces. "You'd get hungry and they'd say, 'Well, it's just the two-
minute warning.' To a kid, two minutes means two minutes, but to a football
game, two minutes means forever."

Like Bzoskie, Mary Peterman, retired now from St. Louis County Social
Services work, was invited to travel with her uncle and the Minnesota Vikings
on the team plane. She attended a tilt in Baltimore. She also tagged along on
the flight to Winnipeg when Haugsrud went to discuss the Vikings' head-
coaching job with his old friend from Superior, Bud Grant.

"There were a lot of trips we were able to take with them," she said. "We
got the benefit of being treated very well. [We] all got to spend a lot of time
with Marge and Ole."

And they got to meet NFL icons like Ernie Nevers and George Halas.
"Those guys were just really old guys to me," said Mary's brother, John Peterman, a mail carrier in Duluth. "I enjoyed the times I had with all those people,
meeting all those people. I realized later it was really neat."

His Uncle Ole "was quiet, but not shy or anti-social," John said. "Everyone
knew him, knew who he was. He was really generous to a fault. He was always
helping people. And he was always telling stories, always talking about the
good old days."

But Haugsrud lived in the moment, too. He arranged for John's eighth-
grade football team to travel to Minneapolis and treated the boys to a Vikings
game. He later helped his nephew become a Vikings ball boy for seven seasons.

"He was always the promoter more than the athlete," John said. "I think
he wanted to be in front of the scenes, but behind the scenes was as close as
he got."

To help out his nieces and nephews, Haugsrud also offered them odd jobs.
Mary remembers stamping the tax onto packs of cigarettes at the canteen
service business or stuffing and addressing envelopes. The children also were
drafted to clean the Haugsruds' boat, which bore the same name as the building that housed their top-floor apartment, the *Rosemar*. The Haugsruds took
their relatives out on the boat every Fourth of July, Mary said. They picnicked
on an island up the St. Louis River they came to call "Potato Salad Island."

~

An honor that managed, somehow, to elude Haugsrud through all the years, and despite all he did for the NFL, and all he meant to the league, was an induction in the Pro Football Hall of Fame in Canton, Ohio. He was named a finalist and a senior nominee in 1973, but his exclusion from the ranks of pro football's greatest remains a travesty.

As longtime *Minneapolis Tribune* sports columnist Dick Cullum wrote in 1975: "Haugsrud has never gotten anything out of pro football but satisfaction. But there is one more thing he deserves. It's a place in the Hall of Fame. He is the only NFL founder who hasn't made it, but he is far from the least deserving. No one has ever had more of his heart in the National Football League."

At the Pro Football Hall of Fame's tenth anniversary celebration in August 1973, charter Hall-of-Fame members—and former Duluth Eskimos players—Ernie Nevers and Johnny Blood McNally agreed that owners shouldn't be enshrined at the same level as players and coaches. "But," McNally clarified, "if they are going to include owners, Ole Haugsrud should be here. He did more for the NFL than Dan Reeves, Charlie Bidwill, and Lamar Hunt combined."

"Amen," replied Nevers.

Bidwill and Reeves were inducted in 1967, Hunt in 1972—why not Haugsrud? His decades of involvement with the league, his ownership of the Vikings, and especially his storied four-year association with the Kelley-Duluths and the Duluth Eskimos craft a convincing case. In a few short years, the Duluth team gained fame from coast to coast. The Eskimos could have argued they were the first "America's Team," had the term been coined.

As Ernie Nevers once said: "Although his name is seldom mentioned along with George Halas, the Rooneys, the Maras, Bert Bell, and other pioneers, Ole was, in my opinion, greatly responsible for the development of early pro football."

The man credited for single-handedly saving the NFL in 1926 ought to be enshrined in Canton.

Loose Ends Laced Up

The story of professional football in Duluth did not end with the Eskimos. In the late 1920s, the Duluth Zephyrs fielded a semi-pro team, and after the Eskimos hit the road in 1926, a Kelley-Duluth professional team continued to play at the western tip of Lake Superior, but not as a part of the National Football League. And like that of Ole Haugsrud, the stories of those who suited up for (and against) the Kelleys and Eskimos didn't end when Ole sold the team in 1927. Many players continued to find work in the NFL, and three—Nevers, Johnny "Blood" McNally, and Walt Kiesling—even made it to the Professional Football Hall of Fame. So for those who are interested, here are some of the loose ends from Duluth's NFL years—all laced up.

~

ESKIMOS IN CHICAGO. When the Eskimos folded, other teams quickly moved to sign its talented players, now without a team. When Ole Haugsrud took a job with the Chicago Cardinals in 1929, so did many of the Eskimos key players, including Nevers, Walt Kiesling, Louie Larson, Russ Method, Bill Stein, and Jack Underwood, and all three of the Rooney Brothers. Mickey McDonnell, who played for Kelley-Duluth, also joined the Cards. That's ten players, plus Uncle Ole and Eskimos coach Dewey Scanlon. Their biggest win—and certainly Nevers' best day on the gridiron—came on Thanksgiving that year.

The field at Comiskey Park was frozen and covered with a slick of fresh snow. Chicago Cardinals' Coach Dewey Scanlon smelled trouble. His team operated out of a double-wing formation that emphasized speed, end runs, reverses, and a bit of offensive trickery. The horrendous footing meant the Cardinals would be able to do little more than play power football. Straight-ahead runs between the tackles.

The conditions seemed to bode better for the Cardinals' opponent, their cross-town rivals, the beefy Chicago Bears. Windy City sportswriters had been hyping the game as a city championship. The two clubs had met earlier in the season, but that grind-it-out, mid-October contest had ended in a 0-0 deadlock. This one was for all the bragging rights.

If power football was required in the rematch, Scanlon had to at least feel a little bit good about the guy who'd handle the ball for the Cardinals on nearly every play: Ernie Nevers. Nevers hadn't played in 1928, the year his Eskimos team had called it quits. He nursed a broken transverse process in his back instead and returned to Stanford to be an assistant coach.

But after signing with the Cardinals for the 1929 campaign, Nevers was back in form. He had been an All-Pro both of his years in Duluth. He was in the midst of the first of three straight All-Pro seasons for the Cardinals. A week before the Thanksgiving Day game with the Bears he had even scored all his team's points in a 19-0 win over the Dayton Triangles. But that performance would be nothing compared to what Nevers was about to do.

About eight thousand shivering fans, most of them from the city's Cardinals-crazy south side, "wanted action," the *Chicago Tribune* reported. They "had waited four years hoping to see the Cardinals sweep aside [their] rivals."

They didn't have to wait much longer. The second time their Cardinals had the ball, Nevers and Mickey McDonnell took turns bulling through the Bears line. Just six minutes into the game, Nevers muscled his way into the end zone from 20 yards out. It would be his longest run of the day. Nevers' boot for the extra point sailed wide, but the Cardinals still led, 6-0.

With time running out on the first quarter, the Cardinals again marched the ball down the field. With All-Pro tackle Duke Slater clearing the way from the three-yard line, Nevers plunged into the end zone a second time. His kick for extra point made the score 13-0.

Smith wrote that in the second quarter, "the Cardinal wave engulfed the Bears." Nevers pushed the ball into the end zone on a plunge play from the six-yard line. The extra point good, the halftime score was 20-0. Three touchdowns and two extra points. Not a bad day's work; but Nevers was only half done.

Early in the third quarter, the Bears finally lit up their side of the scoreboard. With a Walter Holmer touchdown pass to Garland Grange, Red's brother. But the Cardinals immediately went back to work. Nevers answered his opponents' score with a third-quarter touchdown of his own, plunging in from one yard away. He converted the extra point and the score was 27-6.

Ten minutes into the fourth quarter, Nevers scored his fifth touchdown on another one-yard plunge. He ended his day with a ten-yard jaunt late in the last quarter, but missed one of the final two extra points due to a bad snap.

"Then Ernie left the game, and how those south-siders cheered," the *Chicago Tribune'* reported. "Forty points plus nineteen points against Dayton last Sunday gave him fifty-nine in a row. Which is some kind of record, but the south side didn't care. For the Cardinals had defeated the Bears."

Some kind of record? Try the most points in an NFL game for an individual player—a record that still stands today. Years later Nevers called the game his greatest moment in sports, which was saying something.

~

MARION CHARLES "BERT" ASHMORE. After playing nine games for the Eskimos in 1927, the end, guard, and tackle played two years for the Packers, retiring in 1930 at age thirty after twenty games with Green Bay.

~

CHARLES WILLIAM "BUNNY" BELDEN. Belden cut his teeth as a 26-year-old rookie with the 1927 Duluth Eskimos. The fullback, halfback, and quarterback then played eighteen more games and two more seasons—1930 and 1931—with the Chicago Cardinals.

~

PAT BULAND. The native Minnesotan played guard and tackle for the Eskimos for two games in 1926. He later operated the Old Town Bar in Superior and often shared stories of his playing days with his patrons. "He was kind of proud of it," said retired railroad worker Dan Kaluza of Superior, a one-time, part-time bartender at Old Town.

~

OKE CARLSON. The lineman best remembered for devouring twenty-three eggs—and a steak—at a preseason training camp breakfast in Two Harbors, Minnesota, played four years of professional football in Duluth and then spent one season, 1929, with the Chicago Cardinals. Carlson served as a captain in the Army in World War II, and later settled in Remer, Minnesota, where he was in the real estate business and was director of the Remer State Bank. He also was a partner with former Eskimos' owner Ole Haugsrud in Haugsrud's

CCC Canteen Service business in Duluth and was a sales representative for E.I. Du Pont de Nemours Company. Residents of Cass County, Minnesota, elected Carlson to the County Board. Also a member of the Masons, Aad Temple, and American Legion, Carlson died in December 1963 in a Grand Rapids, Minnesota, hospital. He was sixty-two.

~

PAUL FITZGIBBON. Despite being wanted so badly by the Bears' George "Papa Bear" Halas, the "Red-Haired Flash" spent only one year in Chicago. That was 1928. He finished his six-year NFL career with three seasons and twenty-three games for the Green Bay Packers. He retired in 1932 at age twenty-nine.

~

WALLY GILBERT. In addition to playing pro football with the Kelley-Duluth team and the Eskimos in the fall, during the winter Gilbert played professional basketball on touring teams that included the Buffalo Germans, Duluth Tank Corps, Denver Tigers, and the Two Harbors All-Stars who, like the Eskimos, traveled the country to play games. In the spring and summer, Gilbert played baseball. A third baseman, he worked his way through the minors playing in the North Dakota League for Bismarck, in the Western League for St. Joseph in Missouri, in the American Association for Minneapolis, and in the Southern Association for Atlanta. In 1928, he was sold by the New York Yankees to the Brooklyn Dodgers. Over five major-league seasons, including a 1932 campaign spent with the Cincinnati Reds, Gilbert batted .269, including .304 in 1929 and .294 in 1930. One season his fellow Dodgers named him "most popular."

More impressive was his nearly flawless .947 fielding percentage. He played even with the bag, "or even inside it," said his son, John Gilbert, a Minnesota sportswriter. "The game then was line drives and bunts. He would crouch over, on his toes, and his arms would hang full length, swaying back and forth as the pitch was delivered. Apparently, he had cat-quick reflexes, and nothing that he could reach with two quick steps and a dive ever got past him."

When the Dodgers moved to Los Angeles in 1957, *The Sporting News* named Gilbert the starting third baseman on its all-time Dodgers team. "He had to be proud," John Gilbert said, "but he barely acknowledged it, even to me."

In 1937, five years after hanging up his baseball cleats, Gilbert married Mary McKay, a former classmate two years behind him at Duluth's Denfeld High School. A librarian by trade (she was also a singer, dancer, and pianist) McKay used to drive to Chicago with a friend or sister whenever Gilbert's

Dodgers played the Cubs. The couple had a baby girl, Patt, in 1940. John was born two years later. Wally Gilbert was managing the Wausau Lumberjacks, a Northern League affiliate of the Cleveland Indians. "I've already sold him to Cleveland," he joked in the newspaper after his son's birth.

Gilbert returned to Duluth after the 1942 season to work in the U.S. Steel plant, which had increased production for World War II. The following summer, he was "coaxed" into serving as player-manager of the minor-league Duluth Dukes baseball team, his son said. "One of my high school teachers told me that he remembered how my dad would coach third but usually not play until the last inning, coming in to pinch hit during close games," John Gilbert said. "He'd stand at the plate, totally relaxed, and as the pitcher delivered, he'd run up two steps and hit the ball out of the park."

In 1943, Gilbert was diagnosed with an abscessed lung from breathing steel particles at the Duluth Works plant. At the Mayo Clinic surgeons removed the lung, but advised Gilbert's family prior to the surgery that he may not survive. Then they said he wouldn't make it through the night. And then that he wouldn't leave the hospital alive. "They said if he hadn't been such a magnificent physical specimen with a truly amazing heart he never could have survived," John Gilbert said. "He did, and because I was just a baby, I was unaware of the enormous change our family faced. After being so active all his life, my dad couldn't take ten steps in a row or climb five steps without pausing to catch his breath in his one lung. He could never work or be active again." To support her family, Mary Gilbert went to work part-time at her brother Jack's animal hospital and later supervised housekeeping at St. Luke's Hospital.

If Wally Gilbert ever felt bitter about the way things turned out for him, "he never showed it," John said. "I only saw a quiet, soft-spoken side to him, with only extremely rare flashes of temper, and part of that was probably my mom's ability to never complain or make him feel down. Occasionally, Ole Haugsrud, or some former ballplayer buddy who had become a scout, would stop by and there would be lengthy bull sessions at our house. I was too young and too stupid to appreciate the situation or pay attention to the stories."

Wally Gilbert died in St. Luke's Hospital on September 7, 1958, at age fifty-seven, living fifteen years longer than the doctors at Mayo Clinic said he would. Upon his death, the *Duluth News Tribune* wrote that "Gilbert's greatness at virtually any sport he attempted never went to his head. He had an infectious, likable quality to the end.... It would be hard to say that Gilbert was better at any one sport than another as it would be to say whether you liked your right or left arm better."

Eleven years after his death, Gilbert was enshrined posthumously in the Duluth Arena Sports Hall of Fame. Former Minnesota Vikings coach Bud Grant was the speaker. "I'll never forget how Grant said, growing up in Superior, that Wally Gilbert was his idol because he proved you could play with excellence in more than one sport," John Gilbert said. Following the enshrinement, the *Duluth News Tribune* tacked on one more accolade, proclaiming Gilbert "the greatest athlete ever developed in Duluth."

"I'd like to think their spirits are reunited in good times, and I think about them both, every day," John Gilbert said of his parents (Mary Gilbert died in 2002). "Sports stars come and go, and the media hype and hyperbole grow in monumental quantities. As each year passes, the chances are fewer and fewer that anyone will recognize the level of excellence of those athletes from the first three decades of the 1900s, or that somebody from back then might just be the greatest athlete in Minnesota history. Funny thing is, Wally Gilbert probably would prefer it that way. But I know better."

～

ART "THE SWEDE" JOHNSON. Johnson finally left football "because I fell in love and had to go to work," as he explained to the *Duluth News Tribune* in 1963. He had retired a year before that as a railroad sheet metal worker.

～

DOC KELLY. The "Superior Tooth Carpenter" went on to officiate football and basketball games in the Superior-Duluth area. Doc spent five years with both Kelley-Duluth and the Eskimos and later played a major role in attracting the New York Giants to hold training camp in Superior. Active in the community, Doc was a member of Hammond Avenue Presbyterian Church, H.H. Grace Lodge, Elks Lodge, Eagles Lodge, the Happy Home Club, and state and district dental societies. He also was president of the Superior Board of Education. Kelly died of a heart attack suffered in his dental office in February 1954. He was fifty-four years old and left behind his wife Reba and son William.

～

WALT KIESLING. Few linemen in the history of the NFL blasted open running lanes the way Walt Kiesling did. He was the big, burly man up front, the one leading the charge when Ernie Nevers became a star with the Duluth Eskimos—and when Nevers scored his record 40 points in Chicago. In fact, during an illustrious five-year career, the blocker Nevers often followed through the enemy line was "Big Kies," a six foot two, 245-pound legend.

After the Eskimos folded Kiesling played for the 1928 Pottsville Maroons. He then played five seasons for the Chicago Cardinals, earning All-Pro honors in 1929, 1930, and 1932. In 1934 he played with the undefeated Chicago Bears team, one of the best ever in the National Football League. Unfortunately, that team lost the championship to the New York Giants. Kiesling, injured, did not play. The St. Paul native who snubbed Notre Dame for his hometown College of St. Thomas, went to Green Bay in 1935 and in 1936 won an NFL championship with the Packers.

The following season, when Blood McNally went to Pittsburgh as a player-coach for the Pirates, Kiesling went along as an assistant coach. The position launched an unusual twenty-year coaching career for Kiesling. He took over as head coach of the Pirates in 1939 when, according to the Hall of Fame, the always-unpredictable Blood McNally "literally walked off the job." Kiesling continued as coach the following season when Pittsburgh changed its name to the Steelers. In 1941, Steelers' new president Bert Bell made himself head coach. He couldn't win a game, nor could his replacement. Kiesling was back at the helm for the final four games and stayed there—the team's only win coming under Kiesling in the season's final game. In 1943, with their roster depleted due to the war effort, the Steelers merged with the Philadelphia Eagles. The "Steagles," led by co-coaches Kiesling and Earl "Greasy" Neale, finished the 1943 season 5-4-1—just one game out of first place. The following year Pittsburgh merged with the Chicago Cardinals, but with disastrous results. Led by co-coaches Kiesling and Phil Handler, the team lost all ten of its games.

Curly Lambeau then wooed Kiesling to work for him in Green Bay. Kiesling was a Packers assistant for four seasons, returning to Pittsburgh in 1949 as an assistant coach under John Michelosen. In 1954, Kiesling was named head coach of the Steelers once again. Poor health forced his retirement in 1956 with a 40-83 record that did not reflect his coaching skills. "The thing about Walt was that he preferred to be an assistant," Haugsrud once said. "He was available whenever the Steelers needed somebody, yet he would much rather be an assistant than the boss."

Kiesling was a member of the Pro Football Hall of Fame's class of 1966. His involvement with professional football—as a player, head coach, and assistant coach—spanned an incredible thirty years. "The hallmark of Kiesling's career is that he participated in the growth of pro football from its rag-tag days of the mid-1920s to the early 1960s when the sport was bursting with newly won popularity," the Pro Football Hall of Fame boasted. Dick McCann, the hall's first director, agreed. "Walt Kiesling didn't just watch pro football grow from the rocky sandlots. He shoved it along the way. He was one of the game's truly remarkable pioneers."

~

HOWARD KILEY. A colorful lineman with the Kelley-Duluth team for seven games in 1923, six games in 1924, and two games in 1925, Kiley finished his career by playing five games for the Chicago Cardinals in 1926. But he wanted to be part of the Eskimos' barnstorming tour. Hearing that Haugsrud had signed Nevers, he "wired offering his services," Haugsrud recalled. But talking terms with Kiley while he was under contract with Chicago would not have been ethical. Later, a frustrated Kiley called Haugsrud—collect: "Swede, you and Bananas [Dewey Scanlon] put the sugar on the line and I will make the swing with you." Kiley didn't make the swing with the Eskimos. Not officially, anyway. Haugsrud further reported that it seemed Kiley had family in nearly every town the Eskimos played. He would host parties for his former team-mates at his relatives' homes—he just didn't always notify his family first.

~

LOUIS "LOUIE" LARSON. After playing eight games for the 1926 Eskimos, the North Dakota native—a 168-pound fullback, halfback, and quarterback—played three games for the 1929 Chicago Cardinals at age thirty-one.

~

ALLEN J. MACDONALD. Born in Duluth in 1896, the fullback and halfback may have played only one game for Kelley-Duluth in 1923 and six in 1924, but the experience never left him. "They talked about it real favorably, and they talked about Ernie Nevers a lot," said Barbara Murray of Duluth, MacDonald's niece. "I think it was the most significant time in his life."

~

BOBBY MARSHALL. A defensive end for the dismal 1925 Kelley-Duluth team —and one of the first two black men to play in the NFL—Marshall partici-pated in an exhibition game at Nicollet Park in Minneapolis in 1931. That was six years after he stuffed washboards under his Duluth uniform for the last time to protect his ribs. Following his playing days, Marshall worked as a grain inspector for the state of Minnesota. He retired at seventy-eight years old in

1958. He died in Minneapolis in August of the same year. In 1971, Marshall was posthumously inducted into the College Football Hall of Fame. A Milwaukee native, Marshall had been an All-American at Minnesota.

~

JOHN "MICKEY" McDONNELL. The one-time backfield star for Duluth Cathedral High played five seasons in Chicago after newly anointed Eskimos' owner Ole Haugsrud sold his contract to the Cardinals prior to the 1926 season. In 1929, McDonnell called the signals for the Cardinals during Nevers' infamous forty-point day. McDonnell insisted later in life that he was the one who set up most of Nevers' touchdown runs in the game. The *Chicago Tribune*'s coverage suggested his claim probably wasn't far-fetched: "McDonnell swung through huge gaps in the line on delayed plays and dodged his way for long gains," wrote the *Tribune*'s Wilfrid Smith. In 1931 McDonnell signed to play for the Frankford Yellow Jackets. In 1946 he would suit up for both the Brooklyn Dodgers and the Miami Seahawks of the All-American Football Conference, an NFL rival that year. He retired after that season.

~

JOHNNY "BLOOD" McNALLY. McNally's reputation for on-field heroics and off-field antics grew after his days with the Eskimos, with whom he caught thirty passes, scored three touchdowns, and rushed for 250 yards on twenty-two carries. "Johnny always made the difficult play for you," Nevers said. "It was what he did with the easy play that disturbed us. Sometimes, when he was loose on a touchdown run, he might slow down to lateral to a less-swift teammate."

Blood McNally's sometimes-maddening and always-interesting style of play continued in 1928 when he lined up for the Pottsville Maroons, and then for seven seasons after that when he played for Green Bay, helping the Packers to four league championships in 1929, 1930, 1931, and 1936. In 1931, he scored thirteen touchdowns—then a league record—and was named to the all-pro team. The next year he broke the record for touchdown receptions in a season with nine. The "magnificent Screwball" once played nearly an entire game with a collapsed kidney. Packers quarterback Red Dunn recalled one game in which he lateralled to McNally who took the ball fifty yards for a touchdown. Dunn later called the same play, but Blood never moved. "He just stood there an instant with a laugh," Dunn said. "And then threw the [ball] back to me."

Packers owner Curly Lambeau once offered McNally $100 per game—or $110 if he agreed not to drink between Wednesdays and Sundays—game days.

"I'll take the $100 per game," McNally said. Blood would try Curly's patience time and again, often over issues involving money. In Los Angeles he asked Lambeau for an advance on his salary. The coach refused, dead-bolting his eighth-floor hotel room door to ward off the persistent Blood McNally. Lambeau finally gave in after his player scaled a fire escape and jumped six feet to the ledge of Lambeau's half-open window.

In an attempt to keep his unpredictable halfback in check, Lambeau sometimes assigned other players to watch him. But not even the older, more serious-minded Mike Michalske could pull off the assignment. One evening, Blood stayed out past curfew and woke the next morning still drunk. Michalske, in an attempt to hide his failure from Lambeau, suggested that Blood McNally skip practice because he was "too ill." But Blood balked. No way would he miss a practice "for a little thing like bottle flu." Blood couldn't even punt—and Lambeau fired him. It took Michalske and others to get the coach to reinstate Blood.

Lambeau often referred to Blood McNally as "the most fined man in pro football." "He never complained," Lambeau said. "Whether it was for $25 or $200, he'd just say, 'I had it coming, Curly,' and pay."

One season Lambeau resorted to paying Blood just $25 a week and giving him the rest of his salary at the end of the season—provided he stayed off the booze. Blood didn't drink all season—not that Lambeau could tell. "Every day after practice he'd take a couple quarts of milk and go to the home of the editor of the [Green Bay] Press-Gazette," Lambeau recalled. "He had the best library in town. All afternoon, Blood would read books and sip milk." Lambeau's bargain with Blood paid off. "He had his best year, " Lambeau recalled. "He was All-Pro and we won the championship. At the end of the season, I congratulated him personally and gave him the rest of his money, a few thousand dollars that had accumulated." Just a couple weeks later, Blood was broke. He told Lambeau he spent it all on Christmas gifts for his family.

Perhaps the most notorious Blood McNally story happened after the Packers whipped the Bears to win the 1930 NFL championship. They celebrated that night in Chicago's Knickerbocker Hotel, and the party continued the following afternoon as the team rode the rails back home to Green Bay.

"After a while we began horsing around and I started throwing some wet napkins at Lavvie Dilweg," McNally later said. "He didn't like it a real lot and told me to stop. Of course I didn't and he finally got up after me." Dilweg chased McNally through car after car. At the end of the train, Blood got up on the roof of the last car. McNally claims he then said, "So long," to his pursuer and ran back to the front of the train on the roof, jumping from car to car. McNally ran on top of the train all the way to the engineer's cab.

McNally admitted later that the story was exaggerated: he later told historian Ralph Hickok the he ran on the roof of the train only about "seven or eight cars, just far enough to get past the Packers car, and then I came down. I went forward through the cars all the way to the front. Then when we stopped in Green Bay, I got out, ran up to the locomotive, climbed in next to the engineer and let everybody think I'd made the whole trip on top of the train."

In 1932 McNally arrived in camp with a story for the *Milwaukee Journal*. He was flat broke, he told reporter Ollie Kuechle—and needed to get to Green Bay for training camp. He decided to hop a train and ride for free to Green Bay, a trip that required a connection in Amherst Junction, Wisconsin. Though he wasn't a paying passenger, he called ahead to make sure the connecting train waited. While the operators of the connector watched for the passenger who had wired ahead, McNally hopped undetected from one train to the other. The crew—well acquainted with Blood McNally—found him about ten miles outside of Green Bay and quickly ascertained he was the "passenger" they had waited for. According to Blood, the trainman said, "Well, you're the first hobo I ever heard of holding a train for."

"We're going to call you the 'Hobo Halfback,'" Kuechle declared. Blood McNally didn't protest. But Lambeau didn't like it. He didn't think the nickname projected the proper image for his top-of-the-world Packers. "Well, OK," Kuechle relented. "We'll call him the Vagabond Halfback."

In 1933, Blood McNally's days in Green Bay came to an end. Two nights before a game, he was being responsible, but trouble found its way to his hotel room. "I got ready to go to bed, and here two God damned nurses rapped on the door. So my roommate and I ordered up a few drinks," he recalled. "Well, we got pretty loaded. [The] next morning, I went out to practice in not the best of condition." Lambeau sent him back to the hotel and then met him there later. "I've got to let you go," Lambeau said. A year later, Blood McNally was sailing the Pacific as a deckhand.

In 1937, he joined the Pittsburgh Pirates (now the Steelers) as a player-coach, taking over for Joe Bach. He wasted little time in impressing the Pennsylvania faithful, grabbing the opening kickoff of the opening game and sprinting ninety-two yards for a touchdown. In three seasons, Blood McNally compiled a coaching record of six wins and nineteen losses—a dismal mark, the result, possibly, of his inability to shed his wayward ways. "On most teams, the coach worries about where the players are at night. Our players worried about the coach," Pittsburgh owner Art Rooney said.

McNally retired from football in 1939, his forty-five career touchdowns and 270 points —224 of them for the Packers—both NFL records.

"I was reckless, they said, on the football field. Reckless in a lot of things, I guess. I liked to have a good time back then: women, travel, a little drinking. [I] loved to spend money [and] I had a lot of experiences," Blood McNally was quoted as saying in Richard Whittingham's *What a Game They Played*. "I was very uninhibited, that way, all my life."

He served in World War II, joining the Army Air Force in 1941 and working as a cryptographer in China. Not long after being discharged, he married his sweetheart, Marguerite, and ran, unsuccessfully, for sheriff of Wisconsin's St. Croix County. Perhaps the problem was his less-than-serious-sounding campaign platform: cleaning up pro wrestling. He returned to St. John's where he coached football and taught economics and history.

In 1963, Blood McNally was one of the first seventeen players inducted into the Pro Football Hall of Fame in Canton, Ohio. His class included legends like Red Grange, Jim Thorpe, George "Papa Bear" Halas, the Packers' Earl "Curly" Lambeau, the Bears' Bronko Nagurski of International Falls, Minnesota, and of course Blood's Eskimos teammate Ernie Nevers. At the induction ceremony, when it was his turn to take the microphone, Blood didn't thank his teammates or coaches or even his family members. He thanked New York sportswriter Grantland Rice, Arch Ward of the *Chicago Tribune*, and Kuechle. He credited their skill in describing plays and events that he "wasn't quite sure had happened" for his fame.

The man who gave him his nickname perhaps best summed him up:

"John Blood [was] one of the grandest guys in all sports," Kuechle wrote. "Well-read, exceptionally well-read. Wild. Handsome. Unpredictable. As big-hearted as they come and as wasteful both of himself with the wonderful physique nature gave him and of his goods. And a great athlete. He could be one with the riff-raff in a waterfront bar one day then recite Keats, Shelley, or Shakespeare by the hour in different company the next. He could drop a pass thrown right in his hands and then get one that nobody else could."

McNally died November 28, 1985, while spending the winter in Palm Springs, California. He was eighty-two. Known to disappear into libraries with two quarts of milk to study economics for hours at a time, Blood McNally left a book behind when he died. It was not, however, a memoir of his notorious exploits in the NFL, but rather an analysis of the Malthusian theory of population and economics. Unexpected? His widow didn't think so: "Even when Johnny does the expected he does it in an unexpected way," she said.

⁓

RUSS METHOD. *Duluth News Tribune* sports columnist Bruce Bennett once wrote that Method, a Duluth Denfeld High graduate, was "generally agreed to be one of the finest backs ever developed in the city." After five NFL seasons and thirty-five games for his hometown, "Cuss" played ten games for the Chicago Cardinals in 1929. Beyond his success and versatility on the field (he played end, fullback, guard, halfback, and quarterback) the five foot ten inch, 192-pound Method earned a reputation for toughness and reportedly broke his nose fourteen times in six seasons. In addition to football, he played professional baseball in the Northern League for Fargo, North Dakota. A veteran of World War I, Cuss retired in 1962 from Inland Steel Corporation after thirty-three years of service. Method died in a Two Harbors hospital in 1971 while on vacation from his home in Chicago. He was seventy-four.

⁓

ERNIE NEVERS. In 1932, Nevers moved back to California and assumed the position of backfield coach at his alma mater, Stanford. After four seasons, he moved east, taking over as head football coach at Lafayette College in Easton, Pennsylvania. After just one season there, he accepted an offer from his former high school coach, Ira Tubbs, and landed back near his Midwestern roots. He became the head backfield coach for the University of Iowa, where Tubbs was head coach. In accepting the job, Nevers said in an Associated Press interview he rejected "an attractive offer" from the NFL's Cleveland Rams. The NFL beckoned again in 1939, and Nevers answered the call, taking over as head coach of the Chicago Cardinals. But when his team won only one game against ten losses, he resigned and returned yet again to Stanford. This time, though, he was a student, working to complete his physical education degree.

World War II broke out, and even though he was thirty-eight years old—easily old enough to be excused from military service—Nevers volunteered. He signed up for the Marine Corps. He rose in rank to major while serving in the South Pacific as an ordnance officer in the 134th Torpedo Bomber Squadron. While overseas, his wife, the former Elizabeth Heagerty, died. The two had been married nearly twenty years, ever since 1926, the year they drove together from St. Louis to Two Harbors, Minnesota, arriving late for the Duluth Eskimos' training camp.

In 1945, Nevers coached the Chicago Rockets, a brand-new football team for the brand-new All-American Football Conference, another rival to the NFL. But he was looking toward a life outside of football. "There's nothing more in this game," he told sportswriters at the time. "I'm going into business and [will] just help [with football] in my spare time."

Soon afterwards, Nevers met actress Marjorie Luxem Railton on a blind date arranged by friends. He was so taken by her he proposed marriage that very night. Marjorie refused—she didn't know who *the* Ernie Nevers was—but soon came around. A few months later, the two married and moved back to California where they settled in tony Tiburon, an affluent town on the Tiburon Peninsula, which reaches south into San Francisco Bay. There their daughter Ernestine was born. Nevers then took his first non-football job, working in public relations and sales for Sobel Liquors, a wholesale firm.

"For some reason the liquor business and an interest in sports seem to go together," Nevers told the *San Francisco Examiner* in 1964. "My reputation and contacts naturally open doors for me, but once inside, it's the businessman that has to carry the ball." Nevers allowed his football days to fade into memory as he focused on work and a new hobby, golf. "I really don't think too much about football," he said, "but people ask a lot about it. To me, it's a closed book. Part of my past. It was great, but it's over, and I have a full life now. I'm very grateful to what sports have given me, and my memories of those days are very fond, but my life is now—in the present. And I'd just as soon be known as a good businessman. Also, I wouldn't mind knocking a few strokes off my handicap."

The old days did still come up any time former Duluth Eskimos' owner Ole Haugsrud visited the San Francisco Bay area while traveling with his new team, the Minnesota Vikings. But beyond those visits, "football is almost never mentioned," Marjorie Nevers said in 1964. "It's only strangers who bring it up." Nevers even came up with a pat answer any time someone would ask if he was really as good as his legend. "Nope," he'd say, a sly smile crossing his rugged, tanned face. "But the fans are like whiskey—the older they get the mellower they get."

Nevers may have been ready to put football in the past, but football wasn't ready to let go of him. In 1951, he was inducted in the College Football Hall of Fame. In 1962, *Sports Illustrated* magazine named Nevers the best college football player ever. In 1963, the same year he was inducted into the Pro Football Hall of Fame, Nevers was named to the NFL's All-Time All-Pro Team. He was a member of the inaugural class of the Superior, Wisconsin, Athletic Hall of Fame in 1967. In 1969 he was named to college football's All-Time All-American Team, as chosen by the Football Writers Association of America. That same year Nevers was enshrined in the Duluth Arena Sports Hall of Fame with his former Eskimos' teammate Wally Gilbert.

Nevers died of kidney disease on May 3, 1976, in San Rafael, California. He was 73. In his final days, he was "in terrible pain," his wife would say when her husband was inducted posthumously into the San Jose Sports Hall of Fame. "It seemed like every bone in his body had been broken when he played football," Marjorie Nevers said. "In all the years that we were married, I never heard him say an unkind word about someone. He was an incredible human being."

~

DICK O'DONNELL. The Duluth Denfeld High graduate —who worked as an electrician after a stint in the Duluth-Superior shipyards during the first world war—played just seven games for Kelley-Duluth in 1923 before moving on to Green Bay to play seven seasons for the Packers. He retired after playing the 1931 season with the Brooklyn Dodgers.

~

THE ROONEY BROTHERS. The pride of Roosevelt High School in Virginia, Minnesota—and the only three players to play together on the same NFL team during the same season—didn't stop playing football after the Eskimos folded in 1927.

Bill Rooney, who had finished the 1925 campaign with the New York Giants before playing for the Brooklyn Lions in 1926 and then returning to Duluth in 1927, finished his playing career in 1929, suiting up for nine games with the Chicago Cardinals. Haugsrud called him "a mighty backfield man.... whose spectacular performances at Roosevelt High in Virginia had put that institution of learning on the Northwest football map."

After four seasons in Duluth, the last with the Eskimos in 1927, **Cobb Rooney** played two games for the New York Yankees in 1928 and twenty games for the Chicago Cardinals in 1929 and 1930.

Joe Rooney had perhaps the most fulfilling NFL career. He played thirteen games for Kelley-Duluth in 1923 and 1924, ten games for the Rock Island Independents in 1925, twenty-one games for the Eskimos in 1926 and 1927, ten games for the Pottsville Maroons in 1928, and two games for the Chicago Cardinals in 1929. That's fifty-six games and five teams in seven years.

DEWEY SCANLON. The Kelley-Duluth football founder and team manager sat out of the 1928 season. In 1929, he was back, coaching the Chicago Cardinals to a record of six wins, six losses, and one tie. He then settled back in Duluth. In 1944, he was working for the Walter Butler Shipyards in Duluth's Riverside neighborhood when, at the age of forty-five, he died tragically. Scanlon was living with his sister and her husband in Duluth's West End. The couple had gone out, returning around one in the morning. But they were unable to open their front door. A downstairs tenant, Mrs. Arthur Lindgren, called West Duluth Police. Officers forced open the rear entrance. They found Scanlon's body wedged against the front door, his right eye swollen, blood on the floor under his face. After an investigation his death was ruled accidental, the result of a fall down the stairway. What caused the fall remained a mystery. A heart attack, maybe, or perhaps Scanlon lost his balance while reaching for a key on a windowsill at the top of the stairs—The key was found on a top step.

BILL STEIN. The legendary lineman from Two Harbors, Minnesota, played seven bruising seasons and thirty-eight league games for Kelley-Duluth, the Eskimos, and the Chicago Cardinals. He took quite a beating along the way. Stein once told his hometown friend Larry Hurd, "We played with cuts, bruises, and boils on our asses. We didn't dare come out of a game; someone would replace us. We played with bent knuckles, curved knuckles, and scraped knuckles." When his playing days ended, Stein returned to Two Harbors where he became a fixture in the community. He ran the American Legion Post 109 clubroom and worked as a salesman for Superior's Saratoga Liquor. In 1983 at eighty-four years old, he died in his hometown.

JACK UNDERWOOD. Like so many other Eskimos players, the Duluth Central High graduate played for the Chicago Cardinals in 1929. He had also played three games for the Buffalo Bisons and one game for the Pottsville Maroons in 1927.

ROSTERS & RECORDS*

Duluth's NFL Teams' Coaching Records

Name	Team	Year(s) as Coach	Record (W-L-T)
Joe Sternaman	Kelley-Duluth	1923	4-3-0
Dewey Scanlon	Kelley-Duluth, Eskimos	1924-26	11-9-3
Ernie Nevers	Duluth Eskimos	1927	1-8-0

Duluth's NFL Teams' Records v. Opponents

Team	Record Against (W-L-T)	Points Scored	Points Allowed
Minneapolis Marines	4-0-0	28	0
Hammond Pros	2-0-0	29	0
Akron Pros	1-0-0	10	7
Canton Bulldogs	1-0-0	10	2
Green Bay Packers	1-3-1	6	46
Hartford Blues	1-0-0	16	0
Kansas City Cowboys	1-2-0	15	15
Kenosha Maroons	1-0-0	32	0
Milwaukee Badgers	1-1-0	10	12
Pottsville Maroons	1-2-0	27	19
Racine Tornadoes	1-0-0	21	0
Rock Island Independents	1-1-0	9	12
Chicago Cardinals	0-2-0	6	20
Chicago Bears	0-2-0	20	51
Cleveland Bulldogs	0-2-0	20	41
Detroit Panthers	0-0-1	0	0
Frankford Yellow Jackets	0-2-0	0	16
New York Giants	0-2-0	13	35
Providence Steam Roller	0-1-1	7	13

*Records include only league games; exhibition game records are unavailable. "Hometown" refers to the town the player lived in while attending high school, not necessarily the town where he was born.

The 1923 Kelley-Duluth Team

Name	Hometown	Position(s)	Games Played
Roddy Dunn	Duluth, Minnesota	guard, tackle	2
Wally Gilbert	Duluth, Minnesota	fullback, halfback	7
Ira Haaven	McIntosh, Minnesota	end, guard	3
Ken Harris	Duluth, Minnesota	fullback	6
Art Johnson	Duluth, Minnesota	guard, tackle	7
Howard Kiley	Michigan (city unknown)	tackle, guard	7
Allen MacDonald	Duluth, Minnesota	fullback, halfback	1
John Madigan	Madison Lake, Minnesota	center, tackle	7
Russ Method	Duluth, Minnesota	end, fullback, guard, halfback, quarterback	7
Max Morse	Unknown	guard	1
Dick O'Donnell	Duluth, Minnesota	end, halfback	7
Bill Rooney	Virginia, Minnesota	center, fullback, guard, halfback, quarterback	5
Joe Rooney	Virginia, Minnesota	end, halfback, tackle	7
Bill Stein	Two Harbors, Minnesota	guard, center, halfback, tackle	6
Joey Sternaman	Springfield, Illinois	halfback, quarterback	7
Dan Williams	St. Cloud, Minnesota	guard	6

1923 Results, Kelley-Duluth (4-3)

Date	Opponent	W, L, or T	Score
September 30	vs. Akron Pros	W	10–7
October 7	at Minneapolis Marines	W	10–0
October 21	vs. Hammond Pros	W	3–0
October 28	vs. Minneapolis Marines	W	9–0
November 11	at Milwaukee Badgers	L	3–6
November 18	at Chicago Cardinals	L	0–10
November 25	at Green Bay Packers	L	0–10

1923 NFL Final Standings

Team	Record (W-L-T)	Winning Percentage
Canton Bulldogs	11-0-1	1.000
Chicago Bears	9-2-1	.818
Green Bay Packers	7-2-1	.778
Milwaukee Badgers	7-2-3	.778
Cleveland Indians	3-1-3	.750
Chicago Cardinals	8-4-0	.667
Kelley-Duluth	4-3-0	.571
Columbus Tigers	5-4-1	.556
Buffalo All-Americans	4-4-3	.500
Racine Legion	4-4-2	.500
Toledo Maroons	2-3-2	.400
Rock Island Independents	2-3-3	.400
Minneapolis Marines	2-5-2	.286
St. Louis All-Stars	1-4-2	.200
Hammond Pros	1-5-1	.157
Dayton Triangles	1-6-1	.143
Akron Indians	1-6-0	.143
Oorang Indians	1-10-0	.091
Rochester Jeffersons	0-2-0	.000
Louisville Brecks	0-1-0	.000

The 1924 Kelley-Duluth Team

Name	Hometown	Position(s)	Games Played
Oke Carlson	Two Harbors, Minnesota	center, guard, tackle	4
Herb Clow	Duluth, Minnesota	end	1
Art Engstrom	Knox, Indiana	guard, tackle	1
Wally Gilbert	Duluth, Minnesota	fullback, halfback	5
Art Johnson	Duluth, Minnesota	guard, tackle	6
Doc Kelly	Superior, Wisconsin	fullback, halfback	5
Howard Kiley	Michigan (town unknown)	tackle, guard	6
Allen MacDonald	Duluth, Minnesota	fullback, halfback	6
Russ Method	Duluth, Minnesota	end, fullback, guard, halfback, quarterback	5
Bill O'Toole	(town unknown)	guard	1
Bill Rooney	Virginia, Minnesota	center, fullback, guard, halfback, quarterback	6
Cobb Rooney	Virginia, Minnesota	end, fullback, halfback, quarterback	6
Joe Rooney	Virginia, Minnesota	end, halfback, tackle	6
Jim Sanford	Mercersburg, Pennsylvania	tackle	1
Bill Stein	Two Harbors, Minnesota	guard, center, halfback, tackle	6
Lief Strand	Two Harbors, Minnesota	center	6
Jack Underwood	Hinckley, Minnesota	end, guard, tackle	6
Roy Vexall	Minnesota (town unknown)	end, fullback	2
Dan Williams	St. Cloud, Minnesota	guard	6

1924 Results, Kelley-Duluth (5-1)

Date	Opponent	W, L, or T	Score
September 28	vs. Green Bay Packers	W	6-3
October 5	at Minneapolis Marines	W	3-0
October 26	vs. Kenosha Maroons	W	32-0
November 2	at Minneapolis Marines	W	6-0
November 9	at Green Bay Packers	L	0-13
November 23	at Rock Island Independents	W	0-9

1924 NFL Final Standings

Team	Record (W-L-T)	Winning Percentage
Cleveland Bulldogs	7-1-1	.875
Chicago Bears	6-1-4	.857
Frankford Yellow Jackets	11-2-1	.846
Kelley-Duluth	5-1-0	.833
Rock Island Independents	6-2-2	.750
Green Bay Packers	7-4-0	.636
Racine Legion	4-3-3	.571
Chicago Cardinals	5-4-1	.556
Buffalo Bisons	6-5-0	.545
Columbus Tigers	4-4-0	.500
Hammond Pros	2-2-1	.500
Milwaukee Badgers	5-8-0	.385
Akron Indians	2-6-0	.333
Dayton Triangles	2-6-0	.333
Kansas City Blues	2-7-0	.222
Kenosha Maroons	0-5-1	.000
Minneapolis Marines	0-6-0	.000
Rochester Jeffersons	0-7-0	.000

The 1925 Kelley-Duluth Team

Name	Hometown	Position(s)	Games Played
Charlie Black	Alton, Illinois,	end	1
Oke Carlson	Two Harbors, Minnesota	center, guard, tackle	3
Fred Denfield	Duluth, Minnesota	guard, tackle	3
Wally Gilbert	Duluth, Minnesota	fullback, halfback	2
Art Johnson	Duluth, Minnesota	guard, tackle	2
Doc Kelly	Superior, Wisconsin	fullback, halfback	3
Howard Kiley	Michigan (town unknown)	tackle, guard	2
Mike Koziak	(town unknown)	guard	1
Bobby Marshall	Milwaukee, Wisconsin	end	2
Mickey McDonnell	Duluth, Minnesota	fullback, halfback, quarterback	3
Russ Method	Duluth, Minnesota	end, fullback, guard, halfback, quarterback	3
Wally O'Neill	Duluth, Minnesota	end, guard, tackle	3
Bill Rooney	Virginia, Minnesota	center, fullback, guard, halfback, quarterback	2
Cobb Rooney	Virginia, Minnesota	end, fullback, halfback, quarterback	3
Bill Stein	Two Harbors, Minnesota	guard, center, halfback, tackle	3
Sundquist	(first name, Hometown, and position unknown)		1
Jimmy Tobin	(town unknown)	end	1
Jack Underwood	Hinckley, Minnesota	end, guard, tackle	2
Dan Williams	St. Cloud, Minnesota	guard	2

1925 Results, Kelley-Duluth (0-3)

Date	Opponent	W, L, or T	Score
September 27	vs. Kansas City Cowboys	L	0–3
October 11	vs. Rock Island Independents	L	0–12
October 31	at Chicago Cardinals	L	6–10

1925 NFL Final Standings

Team	Record (W-L-T)	Winning Percentage
Chicago Cardinals	11-2-1	.846
Pottsville Maroons	10-2-0	.833
Detroit Panthers	8-2-2	.800
New York Giants	8-4-0	.667
Akron Indians	4-2-2	.667
Frankford Yellow Jackets	5-3-3	.625
Chicago Bears	9-5-3	.643
Rock Island Independents	5-3-3	.625
Green Bay Packers	8-5-0	.615
Providence Steam Roller	6-5-1	.545
Canton Bulldogs	4-4-0	.500
Cleveland Bulldogs	5-8-1	.385
Kansas City Cowboys	2-5-1	.286
Hammond Pros	1-4-0	.200
Buffalo Bisons	1-6-2	.143
Kelley-Duluth	0-3-0	.000
Rochester Jeffersons	0-6-1	.000
Milwaukee Badgers	0-6-0	.000
Dayton Triangles	0-7-1	.000
Columbus Tigers	0-9-0	.000

The 1926 – 1927 Duluth Eskimos Team

Name	Hometown	Position(s)	Games Played
Walt Buland	Minnesota (town unknown)	guard, tackle	2
Oke Carlson	Two Harbors, Minnesota	center, guard, tackle	1
Paul Fitzgibbon	Sioux Falls, South Dakota	end, fullback, halfback, quarterback	13
Walt Gayer	Janesville, Minnesota	tackle	8
Wally Gilbert	Duluth, Minnesota	fullback, halfback	4
Art Johnson	Duluth, Minnesota	guard, tackle	10
Doc Kelly	Superior, Wisconsin	fullback, halfback	5
Walt Kiesling	St. Paul, Minnesota	tackle, guard	14
Louie Larson	Reynolds, North Dakota	end, fullback, halfback, quarterback	8
Jimmy Manion	Winona, Minnesota	guard	10
Johnny McNally	New Richmond, Wisconsin	halfback	12
Russ Method	Duluth, Minnesota	end, fullback, guard, halfback, quarterback	12
Jim Murphy	Russell, Minnesota	center, end, fullback, halfback	4
Jock Murray	Duluth, Minnesota	end, guard	6
Ernie Nevers	Superior, Wisconsin	fullback, halfback	14
Red Quam	Minneapolis, Minnesota	quarterback	1
Cobb Rooney	Virginia, Minnesota	end, fullback, halfback, quarterback	14
Joe Rooney	Virginia, Minnesota	end, halfback, tackle	12
Harry Rundquist	(town unknown)	tackle, center, guard	4
Dewey Scanlon	Duluth, Minnesota	halfback	1
Bill Stein	Two Harbors, Minnesota	guard, center, halfback, tackle	13
Ray Suess	Minnesota (town unknown)	tackle, end, guard	7
Hew Sullivan	Chisholm, Minnesota	running back, guard	1
Jack Underwood	Hinckley, Minnesota	end, guard, tackle	12
Dan Williams	St. Cloud, Minnesota	guard	12

1926 Results, Duluth Eskimos (6-5-3)

Date	Opponent	W, L, or T	Score
September 19	vs. Kansas City Cowboys	W	8-0
October 3	at Green Bay Packers	T	0-0
October 10	at Hammond Pros	W	26-0
October 17	at Racine Tornadoes	W	21-0
October 24	at Chicago Bears	L	6–24
October 31	at Milwaukee Badgers	W	7-6
November 7	at Detroit Panthers	T	0-0
November 11	at New York Giants	L	13–14
November 13	at Frankford Yellow Jackets	L	0–10
November 14	at Pottsville Maroons	L	0–13
November 21	at Canton Bulldogs	W	10-2
November 27	at Hartford Blues	W	16-0
November 28	at Providence Steam Roller	T	0-0
December 12	at Kansas City Cowboys	L	7–12

1926 NFL Final Standings

Team	Record (W-L-T)	Winning Percentage
Frankford Yellow Jackets	14-1-1	.933
Chicago Bears	12-1-3	.923
Pottsville Maroons	10-2-1	.833
Kansas City Cowboys	8-3-0	.727
Green Bay Packers	7-3-3	.700
Los Angeles Buccaneers	6-3-1	.667
New York Giants	8-4-1	.667
Duluth Eskimos	6-5-3	.545
Buffalo Rangers	4-4-2	.500
Chicago Cardinals	5-6-1	.455
Providence Steam Roller	5-7-1	.417
Detroit Panthers	4-6-2	.400
Hartford Blues	3-7-0	.300
Brooklyn Lions	3-8-0	.273
Milwaukee Badgers	2-7-0	.222
Akron Indians	1-4-3	.200
Dayton Triangles	1-4-1	.200
Racine Tornadoes	1-4-0	.200
Columbus Tigers	1-6-0	.143
Canton Bulldogs	1-9-3	.100
Hammond Pros	0-4-0	.000
Louisville Colonels	0-4-0	.000

The 1927 Duluth Eskimos Team

Name	Hometown	Position(s)	Games Played
Marion Ashmore	Aberdeen, Washington	end, guard, tackle	9
Bunny Belden	Chicago, Illinois	end, fullback, halfback, quarterback	6
Potsy Clarke	(town unknown)	halfback, quarterback, tackle	6
Lawrence Cronin	(town unknown)	end, guard	7
Walt Kiesling	St. Paul, Minnesota	tackle, guard	6
Chick Lang	Chicago, Illinois	guard	2
Jimmy Manion	Winona, Minnesota	guard	6
Jack McCarthy	(town unknown)	tackle	8
Johnny McNally	New Richmond, Wisconsin	halfback	9
Bill McNellis	Duluth, Minnesota	fullback, quarterback	3
Russ Method	Duluth, Minnesota	end, fullback, guard, halfback, quarterback	8
Clem Neacy	Milwaukee, Wisconsin	center, end, tackle	6
Ernie Nevers	Superior, Wisconsin	fullback, halfback	9
Bill Rooney	Virginia, Minnesota	center, fullback, guard, halfback, quarterback	9
Cobb Rooney	Virginia, Minnesota	end, fullback, halfback, quarterback	8
Joe Rooney	Virginia, Minnesota	end, halfback, tackle	9
Bill Stein	Two Harbors, Minnesota	guard, center, halfback, tackle	2
Ray Suess	Minnesota (town unknown)	tackle, end guard	9
Shanely (first name & hometown unknown)		tackle, halfback	1

1927 Results, Duluth Eskimos (1-8)

Date	Opponent	W, L, or T	Score
October 9	at Green Bay Packers	L	0–20
October 23	at Pottsville Maroons	W	27–0
October 30	at Cleveland Bulldogs	L	20–21
November 6	at New York Giants	L	0–21
November 13	at Providence Steam Roller	L	7–13
November 20	at Pottsville Maroons	L	0–6
November 26	at Frankford Yellow Jackets	L	0–6
December 3	at Cleveland Bulldogs	L	0–20
December 11	at Chicago Bears	L	14–27

1927 NFL Final Standings

Team	Record (W-L-T)	Winning Percentage
New York Giants	11-1-1	.917
Green Bay Packers	7-2-1	.778
Chicago Bears	9-3-2	.750
Cleveland Bulldogs	8-4-1	.667
Providence Steam Roller	8-5-1	.615
New York Yankees	7-8-1	.467
Frankford Yellow Jackets	6-9-3	.400
Pottsville Maroons	5-8-0	.385
Chicago Cardinals	3-7-1	.300
Dayton Triangles	1-6-1	.143
Duluth Eskimos	1-8-0	.111
Buffalo Bisons	0-5-0	.000

REFERENCES

Books, Articles, and Web Sites

Aubut, Sheldon T., and Maryanne C. Norton. *Images of America: Duluth Minnesota.* Chicago, Ill.: Arcadia Publishing, 2001.

Bennett, Bruce. "Duluth's Contributions to National Sports." *Duluth: Sketches of the Past.* Ryck Lydecker and Lawrence J. Somner, eds. Duluth, Minn.: American Revolution Bicentennial Commission, 1976: 277–288.

Bernstein, Ross. *Pigskin Pride.* Minneapolis, Minn.: Nodin Press, 2000.

Bishop, Hugh E. *By Water & Rail: A History of Lake County, Minnesota.* Duluth, Minn.: Lake Superior Port Cities Inc., 2000.

"Bobby Marshall: A Minnesota Icon."*African American Registry Web site.* http://www.aaregistry.com/african_american_history/2743/Bobby_Marshall_a_Minnesota_Icon_ (accessed August 3, 2007).

"Bobby 'Rube' Marshall: Member Biography." *College Football Hall of Fame Web site.* http://www.collegefootball.org (accessed August 8, 2007).

Carroll, Bob. *100 Great Running Backs of All Time.* New York: Crescent Books, 1989.

——. "A Team Named Ernie." *The Coffin Corner.* Volume IV, 1982. http://www.footballresearch.com/articles/frpage.cfm?topic=nevers (accessed July 28, 2007).

Cope, Myron. *The Game That Was.* New York: Thomas Y. Crowell Co., 1974.

Daley, Arthur. *Pro Football's Hall of Fame.* New York: Scholastic Books Services, 1965.

Database Football Web site. http://www.databasefootball.com (accessed frequently between June and August, 2007).

Davids, Robert L. "Ernie Nevers."
   Unpublished profile written following an author interview of Nevers, December 9, 1965. Provided by the author.

Dierckins, Tony. *Greetings from the Arrowhead, Volume 1, The North Shore and Canoe Country: A Postcard Perspective of Historic Northeastern Minnesota.* Duluth, Minn.: X-communication, 2007

——. *Zenith: A Postcard Perspective of Historic Duluth.* Duluth, Minn.: X-communication, 2006.

"Ernie 'Big Dog' Nevers: Member Biography." *College Football Hall of Fame Web site.* http://www.collegefootball.org (accessed June 15, 2007).

Frederick, Chuck. *Duluth: The City and the People.* Helena, Mont.: American & World Geographic Publishing, 1994.

Gullickson, Denis J. *Vagabond Halfback: The Life and Times of Johnny Blood McNally.* Madison, Wisc.: Trails Books, 2006.

Henry, Jack. "Johnny Blood: The Vagabond Halfback." *Professional Football Researchers Association Web site.* http://www.footballresearch.com. (accessed June 17, 2007).

Haugsrud, Ole. "Professional Football-Duluth Eskimos."

> *Paper read as the program for the annual meeting of the St. Louis County Historical Society. Duluth, Minnesota, November 19, 1963.*

Hickok, Ralph. "On the Road Again…and Again and Again: the 1926 Duluth Eskimos." *Hickok Sports Web site.* http://www.hickoksports.com/history/hb1926eskimos.shtml (accessed June 15, 2007.) *Originally published in* Sports Illustrated, *Sept. 9, 1987.*

> *Other articles accessed on the Hickok Sports Web site:*
>
> *"Duluth Kelleys 1923-25; Duluth Eskimos 1926-27" http://www.hickoksports. com/history/dulutheskimos.shtml. (accessed June 4, 2007.)*
> *"NFL Franchise Chronology" http://www.hickoksports.com/history/nflfranchises.shtml. (accessed June 4, 2007.)*
> *"Minneapolis Marines / Red Jackets" http://www.hickoksports.com/history/minnmarines.shtml. (accessed June 4, 2007.)*
> *"Nevers, 'Ernie' (Ernest A.): Football" http://www.hickoksports.com/biograph/ neversernie.shtml. (accessed June 4, 2007.)*
> *"McNally, John V. Jr. ('Johnny Blood'): Football" http://www.hickoksports. com/biograph/mcnallyjohnjb.shtml. (accessed June 4, 2007.)*
> *"Leemans, 'Tuffy' (Alphonse E.): Football" http://www.hickoksports.com/biograph/leemanstuffy.shtml. (accessed June 4, 2007.)*

"Enshrined: Billy Petrolle." *International Boxing Hall of Fame Web site.* http://www.ibhof. com/petrolle.html (accessed June 8, 2007).

Jenkins, Sally. *The Real All-Americans: The Team that Changed a Game, a People, a Nation.* New York: Doubleday Broadway Publishing Group, 2007.

Johnson, Charles. "Pro Football in Minnesota-Shades of the Past as well as the Present." Publisher and publication date unknown.

> *The work is an undated article published as part of a promotional document in the 1960s, on file at the Northeast Minnesota Historical Center, Duluth, Minn.; the author was the sports editor of the Minneapolis Star and Tribune and a member of the Professional Football Hall of Fame Committee at the time the work was produced.*

Johnson, Chuck. *The Greatest Packers of Them All.* New York: Putnam Publishing Group, 1968.

——. *The Green Bay Packers: Pro Football's Pioneer Team.* Nashville, Tenn.: Thomas Nelson, Inc., 1961.

MacDonald, Dora Mary. *This is Duluth.* Ashland, Wisc.: Paradigm Press, 1999.

Maraniss, David. *When Pride Still Mattered: A Life of Vince Lombardi.* New York: Simon & Schuster, 2000.

McCann, Dick. "Don't Forget Duluth." Canton, Ohio: The Profesional Football Hall of Fame, 1964.

The work is an article published in an unnamed document by the Professional Football Hall of Fame and is on file at the Northeast Minnesota Historical Center, Duluth, Minn.

Murphy, Robert E. "Duluth Eskimos Football Team."

The work is an unpublished article dated July 31, 1980; provided by the author.

National Football League Archives Web site. http://www.nfl.com (accessed frequently between June and August, 2007).

"More extras needed for 'Leatherheads;' filming in April and May in NC." *North Carolina Film Office Web site.* http://www.ncfilm.com/news_detail.asp?id=273 (accessed March 21, 2007).

"Ole Haugsrud: Pro Football Pioneer." Minnesota Vikings Football Club: Minneapolis, Minn., December 4, 1969.

The work is an article provided by James Finks, the vice president and general manager of the Minnesota Vikings Football Club to Don Smith, Director of Public Relations for the Professional Football Hall of Fame, Canton, Ohio. Article and accompanying cover letter on file at the Northeast Minnesota Historical Center, Duluth, Minn.

Peterson, Robert W. *Pigskin: The Early Years of Pro Football.* New York: Oxford University Press, 1997.

Pro Football Hall of Fame Archives Web site. http://www.profootballhof.com (accessed frequently between May and August, 2007).

Professional Football Researchers Association Web site. http://www.footballresearch.com (accessed frequently between June and August, 2007).

Reichard, Kevin. "Pigskin Chronicles." *MPLS.ST.Paul Magazine.* Minneapolis, Minn.: MSP Publications. Vol. 14, issue 11, November 1986, pp. 157-159.

Scott, Jim. *Ernie Nevers: Football Hero.* Minneapolis, MN: T.S. Denison & Co., 1969.

——. "Johnny Blood: The Swashbuckler." *Quarterback Magazine.* pp. 71–75.

Volume number and publication date unavailable; work is on file at the Northeast Minnesota Historical Center, Duluth, Minn.

Singer, Barry. "Football's Fabulous Ernie Nevers." *Lake Superior Magazine.* Duluth, Minn.: Lake Superior Port Cities. Vol. 8, issue 6, November-December 1986, pp. 22-31.

Smith, Don R. *NFL Pro Football Hall of Fame All-Time Greats.* New York: Smithmark Publishers, 1988.

"Team Colors—NFL: National Football League 1922–Present." *Society for Sports Uniforms Research Web site.* http://www.ssur.org/research/TeamColors/Football_Outdoor/NationalFootballLeague/NationalFootballLeague.htm (accessed August, 10, 2007).

Sullivan, George. *Pro Football's All-Time Greats: The Immortals in Pro Football's Hall of Fame.* New York: G.P. Putnam's Sons, 1968.

Superior High School Yearbook. 1921.

Torinus, John. *The Packer Legend.* Neshkoro, Wisc.: Laranmark Press, 1982.

Troan, John M. *Football @ JT-SW.com Web site.* http://www.jt-sw.com/football (accessed May 18, 2007).

Two Harbors 100 Years: A Pictorial History of Two Harbors and Surrounding Communities. Two Harbors, Minn.: Two Harbors Centennial Commission with the Lake County Historical Association, 1984.

Weyand, Alexander M. *Football Immortals.* New York: MacMillan, 1962.

White, Nicholas. "Great Athletes." Publisher and date unknown.

> *The work is an undated article, publication unknown, on file at the Northeast Minnesota Historical Center, Duluth, Minn.*

Whittingham, Richard. *What a Game They Played: An Inside Look at the Golden Era of Pro Football.* Lincoln, Nebr.: Bison Books, 2002.

Winter, John Charles. "Urban Legend: Washington Redskins are the former Duluth Eskimos." *Superior, Wisconsin, Web Resource.* http://www.superiorwi.us/duluth%20eskimo%20urban%20legend.pdf (accessed June 26, 2006.)

Wyatt, Hugh. "Ernie Nevers: Has there Ever been Better?" *Coach Hugh Wyatt Web site.* http://www.coachwyatt.com (accessed August, 2007).

Zimmerman, David. *Lambeau: The Man Behind the Mystique.* Cedar Rapids, Iowa: Eagle Books, 2003.

NEWSPAPERS

Canton Repository (Canton, Ohio)

Capital Times (Madison, Wisconsin)

Chicago Daily News (Chicago, Illinois)

Chicago Sun-Times (Chicago, Illinois)

Chicago Tribune (Chicago, Illinois)

Daily Variety (Los Angeles, California))

Duluth Budgeteer (Duluth, Minnesota)

Duluth Herald (Duluth, Minnesota)

Duluth News Tribune (Duluth, Minnesota)

Duluth News Tribune & Herald (Duluth, Minnesota)

Milwaukee Journal (Milwaukee, Wisconsin)

New Richmond News (New Richmond, Wisconsin)

Oakland Tribune (Oakland, California)

Pottsville Republican (Pottsville, Pennsylvania)

St. Paul Pioneer Press and Dispatch (St. Paul, Minnesota)

San Francisco Examiner (San Francisco, California)

San Jose Mercury News (San Jose, California)

Star Tribune (Minneapolis, Minnesota)

Superior Telegram (Superior, Wisconsin)

The Evening Bulletin (Philadelphia, Pennsylvania)

The New York Herald (New York, New York)

The New York Times (New York, New York)

The Philadelphia Record (Philadelphia, Pennsylvania)

The Providence Journal (Providence, Rhode Island)

Wilmington Star-News (Wilmington, North Carolina)

Author's
Acknowledgments

This project started with four words in the message field of a single e-mail: "Wanna write a book?"

The note was from Tony Dierckins, who, with his X-Communication publishing house, has been doing as much as anyone to preserve and celebrate the rich and wonderful history of Duluth, Minnesota, a great port city on the greatest of the Great Lakes. For launching the possibility of this book, and also for all the suggestions, editing, marketing, and for just plain getting as excited as me about eighty-year-old stories, Tony deserves praise and appreciation. And his freelance staff and interns—including Scott Pearson, Carly Moritz, Suzanne Rauvola, and Eric Faust—deserve prizes.

Not that I'm in any position to hand out prizes.

But if I were, I'd certainly give them also to Pat Maus at the Northeast Minnesota Historical Center; Kris Aho, Maryanne Norton, and all the reference librarians at the Duluth Public Library; John Gilbert, whose father played for the Eskimos and who was gracious enough to share his rich and vibrant memories; the Rev. John Reppe of Two Harbors, who was good friends with Eskimos' center Bill Stein and whose box of memorabilia included a game program signed in pencil by the Green Bay Packers' great wideout Don Hutson (what a thrill for this old Packers fan to see that!); Bob Murphy of Superior, whose years in television left him with a box of his own research materials and even an unpublished paper he authored about the Eskimos and then shared with me; Craig Grau of Duluth, who dropped off his copy of *The Real All-Americans*, and who, I promise, will get it back; Eskimos' owner Ole Haugsrud, whose written recollections of the pioneering days of professional football provided a great starting point; the late Bruce Bennett, the *Duluth News Tribune*'s sportswriter who really should have written this book decades ago (thanks for leaving it for me); *News Tribune* Editorial Page Editor Robin Washington, who supported my undertaking and didn't turn down a single writing "vacation" request; and *News Tribune* Editor Rob Karwath, who similarly supported the project and who granted me unlimited access to the newspaper's archives.

A special prize is owed to Fred Brown of Owatonna, Minnesota, whose father shared stories with him about the Eskimos when Fred was just six years old and growing up in Duluth. At fifteen he started dreaming of writing a book about the team. Fifty years later the book is finally done, and Fred is owed much for inspiration. His prize is awarded with heartfelt thanks.

The people who deserve more than prizes, of course, are the people at home, especially my wife Julie, who recognized how important this project was to me and who mowed the lawn, did all the dishes, and otherwise gave me as much free time as she possibly could so I could write and research and write some more. I could never thank her enough. Nor could I thank enough my daughters—Claire, Charleigh, and Regine—nor any of my family: Mom, Dad, Lori, Ed, Robyn, Lisa, Cheri, Gary, Shelby, Ben, Steven, Troy, Cindy, Brian, Heather, Josh, Tristan, Samantha, Jeremy, Nicole, Aunt Lois, Dr. J.H., Mary, Marge, Randy, John (one of the all-time great football fans), Amy, Kathy, Aunt Janie, and others.

Finally, this book couldn't have been possible without readers hungry for stories about where we come from and who we are, stories of sandlot days and leather helmets, and stories of the past that deserve to be told, retold, and saved for future generations.

No matter how this project started, that's where it has to end, with the readers who appreciate the carefully chosen words and who can't help but wonder—and imagine—what it might have been like.

— C.F., September 4, 2007

ABOUT THE AUTHOR

Raised a Packers fan in Greenfield, Wisconsin, on the south side of Milwaukee, Chuck Frederick is a veteran journalist of more than twenty years. A graduate of Winona State University in Winona, Minnesota, he has written for a number of Minnesota newspapers, including the *Winona Daily News*, the *Daily Journal* of International Falls, and the *Duluth News Tribune*. With a passion for local history, Frederick currently pens a Saturday column for the *Duluth News Tribune* and serves as the paper's Deputy Editorial Page Editor. Frederick is the author of *Duluth: The City and the People* (1994) and contributed heavily to two *News Tribune* book-length publications: *Aerial Lift Bridge: Spanning a Century* (2005) and *Duluth: Then and Now* (2005). He also helped pen *Grandma's Marathon and Beyond* (2006). His writing has garnered numerous awards and honors, and—despite living in Duluth—in February 1995 he was named Citizen of the Month in neighboring Superior, Wisconsin, for a series of stories that helped a toddler receive a life-saving kidney transplant. His brief but memorable silver-screen career consists of a featured role as a race official in the 1994 film *Iron Will*. In addition to writing, Frederick can often be found with his family or on a softball field, in a fishing boat, leaning over a pool table, on a basketball court, or on a golf course. Still holding out hopes of being discovered by a professional baseball or basketball scout while out playing in his yard, Frederick lives in Duluth's western hillside with his wife and three daughters. And although he lives in Minnesota and wrote this book about Duluth's historic NFL team, he still bleeds Packers green and gold. Vikings fans, try not to hold that against him.